Discovering Irish
Butterflies
& their Habitats

J. M. Harding

Brimstone

Published by Jesmond Harding, 2008.
ISBN 978-0-9560546-0-9
Text copyright © Jesmond Harding.
Photographs copyright © Jesmond Harding.
Printed by Walsh Colour Print.
Design and layout by Michael O'Clery.

Front cover photographs: Peacock butterfly and Killarney National Park.
Back cover photographs from left to right above: Brimstone; Dark Green Fritillary; Brown Hairstreak. Centre: Burren National Park. Back cover, from left to right below: Pearl-bordered Fritillary; Small Tortoiseshell; Marsh Fritillary.

This publication has received support from the Heritage Council under the 2008 Publications Grant Scheme.

This book is dedicated to Denise

Contents

Acknowledgements

I acknowledge all the fieldworkers in Ireland who have contributed information to the *Millennium Atlas* and to the Dublin Naturalists' Field Club website 'Butterfly Ireland'.

Several individuals have encouraged and assisted me in my studies. These include Ken Bond, Michael Jacob, John Lovatt, David Nash and Peadar O'Ceallaigh.

Finally, I want to thank my parents, Charles and Jane Harding, my children, Charlie, Andrew and Alexander and my wife, Denise, for everything.

Jesmond Harding
September 2008

Introduction

From the wilds of the northwest in Donegal to the warm southeast in Wexford, from urban Dublin to the karst landscape of north Clare, there are beautiful areas to enjoy the wildlife of our countryside and the butterflies in particular.

This book encourages practical conservation and is a field guide to Irish butterflies and to some of the best sites for them in Ireland. The best photographs are no substitute for seeing butterflies in their natural setting and no medium can fully convey their elegance and the power and finesse of their flight. This guide will help you discover this joy for yourself.

The book is divided in three sections. The first part of the guide is dedicated to conservation, part two deals with the species accounts and the third section is a site guide. The conservation section looks at the management of the countryside generally and nature reserves specifically and active conservation measures which can be applied in your garden, including plant propagation and habitat creation. The species account includes a photograph of each butterfly and gives details of the life cycle and flight period. The site guide describes twenty-eight chosen locations including how to get there, site ownership, access details and habitats. A species list is provided for selected sites and the sites' characteristics are discussed.

Mullaghmore meadows, County Clare

This book is the result of twelve years' work that has entailed the study of wild and captive breeding, extensive study of the literature, recording and monitoring activity, conservation work and travel. Fellow enthusiasts have provided their expertise and encouragement. I hope you enjoy the book.

Butterfly conservation

Continued enjoyment of butterflies is possible only if their habitats are protected and correctly managed. The natural world is complex, dynamic and constantly changing. Therefore conservation must be an active process. There should be careful but active management of nature reserves and Special Areas of Conservation (SAC) and the creation and management of wildlife corridors in the general countryside.

About twenty of our thirty-five butterfly species inhabit the general countryside (as well as the very special habitats). These are referred to throughout the text as **general countryside butterflies.** In recent decades the general countryside has become much less suitable for even common species. Monocultures of Perennial Rye-grass, barley or other cereal crops are green deserts for butterflies and most other wildlife. Application of grassland fertiliser on pastures cause grasses to grow rampantly, eliminating wild flowers and caterpillar foodplants. Severe and regular cutting of hedgerows also eliminates butterfly areas, as does the disturbing trend towards hedgerow removal. Another recent and damaging trend has been the removal of bramble (*Rubus* ssp), Hawthorn (*Crataegus monogyna*), Hazel (*Corylus avellana*), Gorse (*Ulex* ssp) and Blackthorn (*Prunus spinosa*) from hedgerows while leaving taller trees which results in a line of trees, usually Ash (*Fraxinus excelsior*) and Elder (*Sambucus nigra*), looking exposed and naked without the hedgerow shrubs. This destructive process impoverishes the whole ecosystem removing cover and breeding sites for Foxes (*Vulpes vulpes*), Hedgehogs (*Erinaceus europaeus*), Stoats (*Mustela erminea*), birds and insects. It results in more land being brought into cultivation with a massive loss of biodiversity. Further damage is caused by the drainage of damp pastures that eliminates many wild flowers and rich butterfly habitats.

The result of agricultural intensification is a dull countryside with depleted habitats and without colour and personality. We are all poorer because of these losses.

Traditional wet meadow

How to protect butterflies in the general countryside

A well managed flowering hedgerow

A corridor for wildlife should be provided around the margins and corners of fields. A five metre wide strip extending out from the hedgerow should be left uncultivated (in a tillage area) and not have grassland fertiliser applied (in a pasture). Hedgerows should be cut on a rotational basis and outside the March to September period. Hedgerows should in general be two metres high and cut to an 'A' shape. A variety of height could ideally be allowed to develop as different heights suit different species and some species require differing heights for different activities. Thus the Speckled Wood butterfly feeds on nectar from flowering bramble in a sunny sheltered part of the hedgerow but it mates at the top of a hedgerow or high in a tree and lays its eggs on grasses bordering the hedgerow.

By leaving a network of inter-connected strips of land along with the intact hedgerows you are replicating a woodland edge/grassland habitat-conditions that butterflies and many other creatures enjoy best. Habitats would be improved if farmers left damp corners alone and avoided over-enthusiastic mortar repairs to old stone walls. The countryside would benefit from a relaxation of management and a lessening of intensification practices.

Reserve management practice

Reserves are SAC's (areas designated under EU Habitats Directive as Special Areas of Conservation), national nature reserves and indeed any area where wildlife conservation is the primary concern/activity. Many good butterfly sites are within such areas and this would seem to safeguard the butterflies and habitats.

However, this has proved not to be the case in some instances. Putting a fence around a reserve and ensuring it cannot be built on, polluted or damaged is not sufficient to protect the habitats of butterfly populations. The literature is littered with examples of nature reserves from which species have been lost. The Dizzard Reserve, acquired for the protection of the Large Blue in the southwest of England lost the species because burning and grazing activities that ensured the butterfly's survival were stopped. Monk's Wood in Cambridgeshire lost twelve species due to lack of management.

The record in Ireland is also unenviable. The Marsh Fritillary was lost from Ballinafagh and Pollardstown in County Kildare due to the cessation of grazing by horses. The sward grew denser and scrub invaded making conditions unsuitable for this rare grassland butterfly. Maintenance of habitat for butterfly and other invertebrate populations often involves the use of grazing regimes in grassland, coppicing, periodic scrub clearance and ride maintenance in woodlands.

Extensive horse grazing practiced in the Burren National Park

This message has now been clearly understood in Britain but it has yet to be accepted here. Active management is sometimes derisorily referred to as wildlife gardening. One of the factors that has resulted in Irish butterfly populations being more abundant than those in Britain is the fact that Irish agriculture is not as yet as intensive as British farming. However, there are other causes for concern. These concerns lie in the rapid expansion of road infrastructure and towns, one-off housing in the countryside, abandonment of the countryside by small farmers in parts of the west, midlands and southwest, coniferisation of marginal land, destruction of peat bogs and limestone pavement. Unless we ensure that habitats have large enough critical mass and are connected and managed we risk losing more of our heritage.

You can help

Aside from joining conservation organisations there is something that most of us can do to conserve butterflies and other wildlife in our gardens. Many of us have a garden but rather than see our garden as a place where we have to keep the grass cut why not see it as a habitat for butterflies. Most of our general countryside butterflies are mobile and you stand a good chance of attracting them if you change the management of your garden.

Plant nectar-rich flowering plants and shrubs in a sunny, sheltered part of your garden. Shrubs that are especially attractive include Buddleia and Hebe (*Hebe* ssp), while Lavender (*Lavandula angustifolia*), Verbena (*Verbena bonariensis*), Ice Plant (choose *Sedum spectabile*), Marjoram (*Origanum vulgare*), Chives (*Allium schoenoprasum*), Thyme (*Thymus praecox*), Michelmas Daisy (*Aster novae-belgii*) and Grape Hyacinth (*Muscari neglectum*) will attract butterflies, sometimes in remarkable numbers.

Native hedgerow featuring Guelder Rose, Hazel and Irish Whitebeam

Planting a hedgerow, consisting of native plants such as Hawthorn, Blackthorn, Holly (*Ilex aquifolium*), Privet (*Ligustrum vulgare*), Guelder Rose (*Viburnum opulus*), Alder Buckthorn (*Frangula alnus*), Common Buckthorn (*Rhamnus catharticus*), Ivy (*Hedera helix*) and Hazel is an attractive feature for butterflies, especially if bordered by native grasses and wild flowers. A native hedgerow provides places for basking, feeding, resting, roosting, mating and egg laying.

Wildflower lawn

Wildflower lawn

Creation of a wetland associated with a pond and planting this with wetland flowers such as Lady's Smock (*Cardamine pratensis*), Water-mint (*Mentha aquatica*), Fleabane (*Pulicaria dysenterica*), Water-cress (*Nasturtium offinale*) and Purple Loosestrife (*Lythrum salicaria*) is of great benefit to wildlife including butterflies.

Before deciding to create a wildflower garden from the beginning, consider allowing your lawn to grow long and see what happens. Some old lawns are rich in wild flowers but these never have the chance to flower if lawns are mowed regularly. You could allow part of your lawn in a sunny part bordering a hedge to grow long during the summer. You may be surprised to see clover (*Trifolium* ssp), Field Buttercup (*Rununculus acris*) and Ox-eye Daisy (*Leucanthemum vulgare*) appear. These will attract butterflies, bees and hoverflies. A range of wild creatures will be enticed in especially if you allow your wild flowers to set seed. However some lawns are sown with Perennial Rye-grass, a plant that eliminates wild flowers. Application of fertiliser also reduces the chances of wild flowers being present and encourages vigorous grasses that soon crowd out flowers. The best way to create a wildflower meadow when your lawn lacks wild flowers and when your garden soil is too fertile is to create conditions in which wild flowers can thrive. This can be done by removing the top 15cm (six inches) of top soil and using it elsewhere in the garden – for example to build up a bank on which to plant your native hedgerow. Having removed the topsoil, rotovate the soil that was beneath it. If it is stony and sandy, this is good news. Native wild flowers do best in gritty, free-draining soil (although some wild flowers require damp conditions). The best time to do this work is August - early October.

When the soil is fine and crumbly sow native wildflower seed. Seed can be sourced from suppliers whose details are included at the end of this book or you can gather your own. Try gathering fresh local seed as this is more likely to thrive in your garden. The majority of the seed sown should be wild flower seed; sow native grass seed in smaller proportions. Mix the seed with dry sand and sow by the 'broadcast' method, that is, throw handfuls here and there as you judge best. Next, walk over the area and this will push the seed into contact with the soil.

Holly Blue ovipositing (laying eggs) on variegated Holly

For most garden loam soils try a wildflower seed mix consisting of the following: Common Knapweed (*Centaurea nigra*), Field Scabious (*Knautia arvensis*), Devil's-bit Scabious (*Succisa pratensis*), Wild Carrot (*Daucus carota*), Bird's-foot-trefoil (*Lotus corniculatus*), Red Clover (*Trifolium pratense*), Selfheal (*Prunella vulgaris*), Lady's Smock, Ox-eye Daisy, Black Medic (*Medicago lupulina*), hawkbits (*Leontodon* ssp), hawk's-beards (*Crepis* ssp), Common Dandelion (*Taraxacum officinale*), Yellow Rattle (*Rhinanthus minor*), Cowslip (*Primula veris*) and Primrose (*Primula vulgaris*). These species will provide colour and attract butterflies from March to October.

Cut the meadow at no lower than a 10cm (4 inches) setting on the lawn mower until May and then allow some of the meadow to flower all summer long. Continue to cut some areas on a 10 cm setting to provide a variety of sward heights to cater for a range of species. Mow a path through the meadow for access and enjoyment. At the end of the season in September, mow or strim the meadow and remove all the cuttings to a compost heap. Do not allow the cuttings to lie on the meadow as these will hold fertility and promote vigorous grass growth. Leave some patches uncut, as they will provide refuge for insects, butterfly larvae and eggs.

Here are some tips that can make a huge difference to butterflies that visit your garden

• Water flowering plants in hot weather. This will increase their nectar content, which may be in short supply during drought.
• If you have a bare patch of soil (for example in a recently dug vegetable patch) spray this heavily with water in the early morning. Male Holly Blues, Wood Whites and Green-veined Whites will drink the dissolved mineral salts.
• Keep some pots of female Holly plants, either the native *Ilex aquifolium* or variegated varieties, and place in full sun against a wall or hedge. Holly Blues will lay on them, with you centimetres away.

- If you have some Ice Plants in pots move these around in early September so they are always in the sun. Butterflies need their flowers to be in sunny conditions.
- Do not trim back dense Ivy. Brimstone butterflies will use it for hibernation and the late summer/autumn generation of the Holly Blue will use it for breeding if it is allowed to flower.
- A log pile in a shaded, wooded part of the garden could be used as a hibernaculum by Peacock butterflies.
- A wooden garden shed with the door or window left open in September/October will certainly attract Small Tortoiseshell butterflies prospecting for a winter hibernation spot. But make sure that they can leave in March.
- A gap in stonework or a small gap in a wall vent allows access to the hibernating Small Tortoiseshells so don't be in a hurry to make unnecessary repairs.
- Allow over-ripe plums to lie on the ground when they drop from a tree; Red Admirals will feast on them.

Female Silver-washed Fritillary on bramble

The golden rule when planting a hedgerow, meadow or developing a wetland is to "think native". Most native butterflies breed only on native trees, shrubs, herbs and grasses. Adult butterflies are not particular about whether their nectar is derived from native sources but they are very specific about larval foodplants.

Butterfly benefits from habitat creation

There is no doubt that gardens can play a role in providing a place for butterflies to feed and breed if the right habitats and food are provided. In my garden there is a flowering herb bed, a woodland edge, a pond/wetland, native hedgerows and wildflower meadow - all crammed in to about one third of an acre. I have a nettle patch in a sunny, sheltered corner for the Vanessid family (e.g. Red Admiral) many of which breed on nettles.

The results have been dramatic. In 2006 my garden, which I developed from scratch, was eight years old. I saw 17 butterfly species in my garden that summer. The number of individual butterflies seen can be enormous. On one hot day in late June there were 49 butterflies in the meadow feeding chiefly on Rayed Knapweed (*Centaurea nigra nemoralis*). By replicating a woodland clearing consisting of a wildflower meadow sheltered by a copse on the north facing side of the garden and hedges facing south and east, a sheltered, warm microclimate has been created- ideal conditions for most native butterflies.

The butterflies that graced the garden in the summer of 2006 were Réal's Wood White, Orange-tip, Small White, Large White, Clouded Yellow, Green-veined White, Holly Blue, Common Blue, Small Copper, Red Admiral, Small Tortoiseshell, Peacock, Painted Lady, Silver-washed Fritillary, Speckled Wood, Ringlet and Meadow Brown. The total of seventeen included two surprises, Réal's Wood White and Silver-washed Fritillary. The former usually frequents tussocky grassland with plenty of trefoils and vetches, its larval foodplants. Was it attracted to the tussocky meadow in the garden that had plenty of Bird's-foot-trefoil, or was it just a wanderer, stimulated to move by a colonising instinct or the hot weather?

Growing 'butterfly friendly' flowers from wild seed

The following native flowers are easy to grow and most are valuable sources of nectar. Some are also larval foodplants.

Foodplant	Latin name	Butterfly larvae	Nectar source
Devil's-bit Scabious	*Succisa pratensis*	Marsh Fritillary	Yes
Field Scabious	*Knautia arvensis*		Yes
Common Knapweed	*Centaurea nigra*		Yes
Bird's-foot-trefoil	*Lotus corniculatus*	Réal's Wood White, Wood White, Common Blue, Dingy Skipper, Green Hairstreak	Yes
Violets	*Viola* species (ssp)	Pearl-bordered Fritillary, Dark Green Fritillary, Silver-washed Fritillary	Yes
Primrose	*Primula vulgaris*		Yes
Autumnal Hawkbit	*Leontodon autumnalis*		Yes
Cuckoo Flower	*Cardamine pratensis*	Green-veined White, Orange-tip	Yes
Kidney Vetch	*Anthyllis vulneraria*	Small Blue	Yes
Stinging nettle	*Urtica dioica*	Small Tortoiseshell, Peacock, Red Admiral, Painted Lady, Comma	
Dandelion	*Taraxacum officinale*		Yes
Thistles	*Cirsium* ssp	Painted Lady	Yes
Ragged Robin	*Lychnis flos-cuculi*		Yes

Devil's-bit Scabious

Field Scabious

Devil's-bit Scabious
This plant will grow in damp and dry situations. Gather seed from seed heads of Devil's-bit Scabious in September just as they are about to disintegrate. Rub the seed head between thumb and forefingers - if it disintegrates readily the seed is ripe for harvesting. If the plants are to be sown in pots, fill the pots with peat substitute or with a mixture of fine gravel and soil (50:50). Ensure the pots are soaked and the surface is level. Then sprinkle the seeds on top and press the seeds in firmly. The seeds can also be sown on an open area in soil that is fine, crumbly and damp. They can also be sown in a gravel driveway/path if the gravel is finely crushed. Always sow fresh seed. Keep pots moist and water from below.

Field Scabious
This plant prefers well-drained soil. Follow the sowing advice given for the Devil's-bit Scabious but allow the substrate to dry out a little. When the plants are of sufficient size plant them on a dry bank that receives good sunlight.

Common Knapweed
This plant (pictured on pages 28, 31 and 59) will grow in most garden loams as well as on peaty and gravelly soil. Extract the ripe brown seed from the flower head by dislodging the seed with your fingernail. Follow the sowing advice given for the previous species and sow the seed fresh. It grows rapidly and could flower the following summer.

Bird's-foot-trefoil

Ragged Robin

This beautiful pink wetland flower grows in damp soils and provides a good nectar source for several butterflies. Extract the seed by crushing the seedpod and scatter on damp soil, pressing down on the seed with the palm of your hand.

Ragged Robin

Primrose

Primroses

Collect seed from ripe pods. Seeds are round, black and sticky and attract the attention of ants. You can prolong the flowering and therefore seed production by 'dead-heading' some of the flowers. Place pots with garden soil mixed with leaf mulch in a shaded position (preferably with dappled shade). Sprinkle seed onto a pre-wetted surface and press them into the soil. Keep pots moist. Alternatively sow fresh seed directly onto fine crumbly woodland soil. Germination occurs after a few weeks.

Violets

Violets

Collect seed from ripe pods in early summer – June is usually a good time. Follow the sowing advice given for the Primrose. Germination occurs after a couple of weeks.

Hawkbit growing among meadow grasses

Hawk's-beards /Hawkbits /Common Dandelion/Thistles

Collect winged seeds from May onwards. Detach from wings and sow onto a gravelly surface, gravelly soil or fine garden loam. Marsh Thistle (*Cirsium palustre*), the foodplant of the Painted Lady, grows best in damp soil and will appreciate peaty soils. Place in full sun.

Marsh Thistle

Cuckoo Flower with male Orange-tip butterfly

Lady's Smock/Cuckoo Flower

Lady's Smock (also known as Cuckoo Flower) is available from garden centres. Its seed can be sown in pots of previously soaked garden soil/peat. Extract seed from pods in June/July and sow by pressing into soil but without burying the seed. Place in full sun but keep the growing medium moist. Germination occurs quite quickly.

Kidney Vetch

Kidney Vetch

Collect seed from disintegrating seed heads in July. The seed is small, hard and black in colour. Sow into pots of sandy or gravelly soil and place in full sun. It will flower within two years.

Two Peacock butterflies ovipositing on the underside of a nettle leaf

Stinging Nettle

Dig around a clump of nettles and cut some pieces of root. Plant the pieces of root directly in the garden in a sunny position under 2cm of garden loam. It thrives best in rich soils, often near a wall or base of a hedgerow.

Growing 'butterfly friendly' trees from seed

Trees that benefit butterflies or their larva are easily grown, although some require patience. The following are valuable nectar sources and/or larval foodplants.

1. Alder Buckthorn (*Frangula alnus*) – Brimstone larvae
2. Blackthorn (*Prunus spinosa*) – Brown Hairstreak larvae
3. Hazel (*Coryllus avellana*) – moth larvae/shelter
4. Holly (*Ilex aquifolium*) – Holly Blue larvae
5. Oak (*Quercus robur/ Q. petraea*) – Purple Hairstreak larvae

Alder Buckthorn showing ripe (black) and unripe fruit

Alder Buckthorn
This scarce plant is the larval foodplant of the Brimstone butterfly and if it were more widespread the range of the butterfly would certainly expand. Although it is usually found growing in acid soil in the wild it grows successfully in garden loams. From late summer (from late July onwards until early November) gather the black, glossy berries. Crush them under water and extract the seed. Sow the seed by pressing them into the surface of damp peat placed in a shallow seed tray. Germination is usually very reliable and will occur the following spring, probably in April. Remove from the seed tray after a month of growth and plant each sapling into individual pots with garden compost or peat substrate with slow release fertilizer granules. If placed in a sunny situation growth is rapid. It will reach a metre or higher in two years and the plant will flower and produce fruit in its second year. It reaches a mature height of c.4 metres.

Blackthorn

This common hedgerow plant reproduces by seed and by vegetative means. Plants send out lateral roots that extend a short distance (often about ½ metre) from the parent and then produce a new plant. This new plant can be transplanted by severing the root connecting it to the parent plant and digging carefully around the young sapling to remove it from the ground. Re-plant immediately in good, well aerated soil. Wait until after leaf fall before digging up any deciduous tree or shrub. Alternatively, collect sloe berries in autumn and remove the seeds. Place a 50:50 sharp sand/compost mixture in a shallow seed tray and water well. Mix seeds in with this (ensuring that all seeds are covered by the substrate) and await germination, which could require the passing of a second winter. Keep outdoors in an exposed position so as to allow the winter cold to get at the seed tray. Nurseries often sell Blackthorn saplings sometimes at low cost.

Hazel

Crack the outer coating (shell) when this is pale brown- this is usually in September. Remove the nut and sow in a shallow seed tray with a mixture of garden loam and sharp sand (not builder's sand) at a ratio of 70:30 respectively. Place each nut about 1cm below the surface and apply protective netting if mice are a problem. Like all the native trees and herbaceous plants described here, ensure the tray is left outside in an exposed position. This is to allow the cold weather to break down the seed's resistance to germination. Germination occurs the following spring. When your seedlings are large enough, transplant into pots and follow the advice given for oak. Hazel is an excellent hedgerow or woodland edge/under storey plant.

Holly

Collect red berries in early December and crush to remove the seeds. Sow the seeds and treat as described for Blackthorn. Germination always takes two winters to accomplish. When your precious long-awaited seedlings have germinated, avoid over-watering the compost and at the first sign of damping off disease (drooping leaves, blackening stalks) spray with a copper fungicide. When the seedlings produce the first prickly leaves transplant to a garden trough or pots containing a good rich compost or peat substitute with slow release fertilizer. Placing the seedlings in a warm position near a south-facing wall can speed up growth considerably. Keep the plants in pots for three or more growing seasons and then plant in their final positions. Plants become fertile after about six years.

Oak

Gather acorns in late September/October and sow immediately in pots of good garden loam. Place the acorn horizontally and cover with 2cm of soil. Germination occurs quite quickly and next spring, you will see your seedling oak send up its first shoot. After a season in the pot plant the saplings into a bed of garden loam.

Oak

Points to Note

1. Watering is preferably done from below, using capillary matting or by placing pots in saucers.

2. Do not allow compost to become too wet (excepting Cuckoo Flower, which will tolerate this).

3. Never allow compost to dry out.

4. It is best to place the resulting plants into their final positions the following spring (March) rather than to try to maintain them in pots. Plant in drifts so that you can have a colour continuum.

5. Sow in the correct place i.e. Cuckoo Flower in marshy conditions or wet grassland, Kidney Vetch onto a fine gravelled drive or sunny dry bank with short, open turf, etc.

Species

FAMILY – HESPERIIDAE

Dingy Skipper Donnán

(*Erynnis tages* subspecies *tages/Erynnis tages* subspecies *baynesi)*

Male Dingy Skipper *baynesi* form

This dowdy, moth-like early summer butterfly is the only native skipper and was until recently the only skipper found in Ireland. It is uncommon and hard to find because of its small size (29mm wingspan) and colour. Sexes look identical and are patterned with greyish-brown. The Dingy Skipper occurs in two forms in Ireland: in the subspecies *baynesi* the light markings are very pale grey, almost white in some specimens. *Baynesi* occurs in the Burren region in Counties Clare and Galway. The subspecies *tages* is found elsewhere in Ireland and its pale markings are somewhat darker. The Dingy Skipper rests frequently on bare patches of soil or rock or, in gloomy weather, on the previous summer flowers' seed heads. It is found from late April/early May to the end of June, but it declines quickly after the first week of June. (In northern France it is double-brooded and may fit in a second brood in Ireland if the climate warms as expected).

It is a fast flyer and skips in rapid bounds and is therefore hard to keep in sight. The adult butterfly feeds on Bird's-foot-trefoil and other spring flowers and when feeding it is easier to observe. It occupies habitats with bare ground or rocky outcrops where its larval foodplant, Bird's-foot-trefoil, is present. Thus it frequents quarries, eskers, limestone grassland and even cut-away bogs. Surprisingly it is not found at many coastal sites and is much less common than its foodplant's distribution suggests it should be. The Common Blue, which also uses Bird's-foot-trefoil as its main foodplant is far more common. It is a largely sedentary species and despite its rapid darting flight, it seldom travels far. Should you be able to train your eye to follow a Dingy Skipper in flight, you will find that it lands a short distance from where it took flight.

Female Dingy Skipper subspecies *tages*

Males searching for females adopt a different flight pattern; they quarter very low over grassland vegetation, maintaining a fussy, flickering wing beat pattern as if concentrating very carefully. They will travel back and forth over the same patch of trefoil-rich turf and are possibly attempting to locate a female by scent. On other occasions males perch and dart forth to investigate any passing Dingy Skipper, returning if their enquiry fails to yield a female.

Single eggs are laid on the upper surfaces of small tender leaflets that represent the most nutritious part of the plant. The bun-shaped egg is very pale green when laid and turns orange later. It hatches after two weeks and the green caterpillar that emerges is a familiar tube-shape. It forms a tent by spinning trefoil leaves together and it lives and feeds within this, spinning a new nest when needed. When fully grown in August it forms a hibernaculum by spinning a denser web over vegetation. It pupates the following April and the pupa lasts about a month.

This species is found chiefly in Counties Clare and Galway and from east County Mayo to County Kildare where it has colonised some cutaway bogs. It is also recorded from Counties Donegal, Sligo, Limerick, Tipperary, Wexford, Waterford, Wicklow and limestone regions in County Fermanagh.

Wood White Bánóg Choille
(Leptidea sinapis)

Wood Whites, (male above, female below)

For years lepidopterists pondered the mystery of why the 'Wood White' was so common in Ireland in fairly open even unwooded habitats while in Britain it was so rare and confined to very specific woodland/scrubland habitats. In 2000 the Ulster Museum explained the mystery – the butterfly found in most of Ireland is Réal's Wood White, a species unknown in Britain, but known in France. The Réal's Wood White is named after Pierre Réal who discovered it on the continent. The Wood White appears to be found west of Athenry in County Galway and certainly in the Burren. It thrives only under critical conditions of light and shade – its larvae need their vetches to have certain precise conditions of sunlight and shade which are met among the Hawthorn, Hazel and Blackthorn scrub of the Burren, where the butterfly is quite common – assuming that all the 'Wood Whites' found there are, in fact, *Leptidea sinapis*.

Its life cycle is similar to that of the Réal's Wood White and it has a small second brood that can be seen in the Burren throughout July and early August. The Wood White is not found in open areas and stays close to scrub, woodland and hedgerows. It may be Ireland's most range-limited species but its identity can only be determined by examining the genitalia of specimens under magnification. Its conservation is therefore a matter of concern.

Réal's Wood White Bánóg Choille Réal
(Leptidea reali)

Male Réal's Wood White

Réal's Wood White was only discovered in 2000 as being an Irish butterfly. Up to that time Ireland was thought to have only the Wood White. Both species are indistinguishable in the field but their genitalia are different and they are clearly a different species. This is a dainty, delicate colonial species with a slow, weak, fluttering flight. It always rests with its wings closed. It has spotless, milky white wings and somewhat darker undersides. The underside of the hindwing is tinged with pale green. The sexes are almost identical in appearance but the male has more extensive black wingtips than the female. The only obvious distinguishing feature is the presence, in the male only, of a white spot on the antennae club. It has a wingspan of c.42mm.

Unlike the Large, Small and Green-veined Whites it is not a butterfly of the general countryside but it is quite common where damp, tussocky grassland occurs. It is common on wet woodland rides, woodland clearings, flower-rich verges with dense grass tussocks, vegetated cutaway bogs, the edges of fens and bogs and unfertilised grasslands such as some lowland commonages.

It is on the wing from about mid-May (although it can appear as early as late April, given a warm spring) to early July and usually has one brood. A very small second brood may fly in late July. Its favourite nectar sources are Bird's-foot-trefoil, Bush Vetch (*Viccia sepium*) and Meadow Vetchling (*Lathyrus pratensis*). Males also engage in an activity known as 'puddling' – which means they congregate on the edges of muddy puddles, imbibing mineral salts dissolved in the water. This activity is usually observed during hot weather.

Despite its weak flight, males remain buoyant for a considerable period of time searching assiduously for a female. A mated female signals her rejection by flapping her wings in irritation. When a virgin is found a remarkable, almost comical performance ensues. The male alights opposite the female, usually on a flower. He faces her and uncoils his proboscis and sways his head from side to side, literally with his tongue hanging out. Suitably impressed, she bends her abdomen to meet his, and copulation follows. The pair remains stationary on the flower head for about half an hour while mating occurs.

In Ireland the plant most frequently favoured for egg laying is Bird's-foot-trefoil, although Tufted Vetch and Meadow Vetchling are also used. A single egg is laid on the underside of a tender leaf. The larva, which is green with a yellow lateral stripe, feeds until mature and pupates low down in a dense tangle of vegetation. When the Réal's Wood White and Wood White emerge from the pupa the pattern is the same. The newly hatched butterfly crawls up a plant stalk, usually early in the morning and dries its wings. It is possible that its emergence is synchronised as large numbers of both species of Wood White emerge at the same time.

The Réal's Wood White is quite common in most parts of Ireland including Northern Ireland but there seems to be a point west of Athenry, County Galway where the Wood White replaces it. Réal's Wood White, while not a general countryside butterfly, is common in suitable habitats and is not as sedentary as its relative. Individuals do wander and have been observed crossing roads and farmland where no suitable habitat occurs.

Clouded Yellow Buíóg Chróch
(Colias croceus)

Female Clouded Yellow on Red Clover

The Clouded Yellow is a fast flying mustard coloured butterfly and it is impossible to keep pace with it if the individual is migrating. When it has settled in an area however, it can be seen fluttering between nectar sources, especially clover (*Trifolium* ssp). The wingspan is up to 58mm in the male and 62mm in the female. The males and females always rest with closed wings so the only certain method sexing the butterfly in the field is to catch and examine it. Hold the thorax between your thumb and forefinger, thereby holding the wings open. The female's black border around the wing margins is punctuated by yellow spots; the male's is pure black. There is a pale striking whitish form called helice – only females occur in this form.

The female lays her yellow eggs singly on the flowers of clovers and a dull green larva emerges after about a week. A yellow stripe punctuated by red at segmental intervals runs along the sides of the caterpillar's body. A greenish-yellow pupa is formed after a larval stage lasting about six weeks and just over a week later the adult emerges. Adults will continue to breed late into October but these attempts fail to survive our cooler conditions later in the year.

This butterfly's occurrence varies from year to year. They are most frequently seen on the south coast but in years of abundance can be found throughout the country. Warm cyclonic conditions from April to September enable many of them to make the journey from continental Europe to Ireland. The year 2000 was a good 'Clouded Yellow Year' as was 2006. In good years the butterfly is seen in places as far apart as Counties Wexford, Meath and Clare, and in abundance.

While not as regular in their appearance as our other notable migrants, the Painted Lady and Red Admiral, they are beautiful and welcome visitors and often harbingers of a good summer.

Brimstone Buíóg Ruibheach
(Gonepteryx rhamni subspecies *gravesi)*

Male Brimstone on Spear Thistle

This large, striking butterfly (wingspan up to 74mm) is especially evident in April and May, when mating and egg laying takes place. The male is very conspicuous as luminous yellow wings flash along hedgerows and woodland edges. The female is pale green and when seen on the wing in bright light resembles the Large White. When landed both sexes keep their wings closed, revealing the remarkable venation that enables them to imitate leaf cover when they roost or hibernate. Flower-rich woodland edges, rides and clearings are its main habitats.

The Brimstone butterfly nectars avidly on a range of flowers, especially in the months preceding hibernation. There is one brood a year, lasting most of the year. It can be seen in almost every month, except for July, when it is scarce. The Brimstone hibernates as an adult, disappearing in September and hanging itself up for the winter in clumps of Ivy or Holly. It emerges as early as February but reliably on warm March days. Its appearance on warm early spring days is heartening as one can see it bouncing joyfully when the sun is shining. It is vigilant and guards itself against a return to winter by immediately seeking shelter the moment the sun is obscured.

Female Brimstone on Common Knapweed

A curious habit of the Brimstone is that it roosts as early as 3 pm in the summer. It awakes about 9.30am. In spring Brimstones enjoy the nectar of Primrose, Common Dandelion and vetches, while in the summertime they visit Purple Loosestrife, Common Knapweed, Devil's-bit Scabious and Buddleia, spending long periods drawing nectar from these flowers. Sometimes pollen becomes stuck to its proboscis. Butterflies find this irritating and Brimstones attempt to dislodge pollen by rolling and unrolling (coiling and uncoiling its proboscis), by dabbing it against a flat surface or by plunging its proboscis between Buddleia florets.

When the adults emerge from hibernation they feed and males seek females. Mating occurs only in spring. Females lay on only two related species of small tree, Common Buckthorn and Alder Buckthorn. Females do not show a preference for either plant species; they lay eggs on both when the two plants are side by side as they are in Lullymore, County Kildare and in the Burren National Park, near Lough Gealain, County Clare. Females lay single eggs on the underside of the leaves or on twigs beside unfurled leaves. The bottle-shaped eggs are green initially, later primrose yellow. The females choose the shrub very carefully and take great care to lay not only on plants in sheltered sunny conditions, but also on the right species. When leafless, females flutter around them to distinguish between buckthorns and adjoining shrubs such as Blackthorn. Females can be observed brushing their wings against the twigs and probably identify the leafless plants by scent. Females also test twigs by alighting on them, fluttering while doing so. If the twig proves to be a buckthorn a single egg is deposited. Eggs are laid over a long period from the end of April to mid-June. The literature gives the hatching time as one to two weeks but in 1996 a very cold May resulted in eggs observed taking twenty-two days to hatch. Eggs turn pale grey prior to hatching.

Mature Brimstone larvae consume entire leaves

The young larva feeds on the centre of the leaf, often staying underneath it. Later the larva eats the leaf from the edge, eating large curved bites, especially the delicate uppermost leaves. When nearly full-grown the rather sedentary caterpillar will devour entire leaves and will sit on the upper surface. Although green in colour, this choice of sitting spot seems to make the creature very vulnerable to predation by birds and wasps. One Alder Buckthorn that received a very large number of eggs produced very few fully-grown larvae. The large wasps observed scouring this shrub were the likely cause of this dearth of mature larvae.

The first captive larva observed pupating did so in late June. It attached itself to a twig by a silken girdle attached to its thorax and a pad on the end of its abdomen – like other Pierids. Larvae about to pupate turn lime-green, the colour of fresh buckthorn leaves. The pupa also has this colour and is placed on the underside of buckthorn leaves and is very well camouflaged. Pupae vary in length from 20-24mm. The pupae are widest at the thorax. By early July the pupa changes from pale green to pale yellow and then, on the day of emergence, to deep yellow with the dull red markings of antennae clearly visible. The adult emerges and hangs upside down on the empty pupa while the wings dry. The pupal stage lasts about fifteen days. Most Brimstones emerge later in July or August. They then seek out flowering meadows to feed up for their long winter sleep.

The Brimstone is not a common butterfly in Ireland. This is because of the absence of its foodplants from many areas. (Alder Buckthorn is a rare plant in Ireland, usually found on boggy soils while Common Buckthorn is found on lime-rich soils.) The Brimstone is found in parts of the midlands and west and is only really common in the Burren. It is rare in Ulster and is no longer found in Northern Ireland. The planting of buckthorns in public parks, gardens and along motorways would, if undertaken, increase its range.

Large White Bánóg Mhór
(Pieris brassicae)

Male Large White (spring generation)

This large Pierid (wingspan generally up to 63mm, but sometimes larger, up to 76mm in the female) appears to be a larger version of the Small White. Apart from the size difference, another distinguishing feature lies in the darker wing tips of the Large White and the absence in the male of a clear spot on the upper surface of the forewing (the female has two prominent forewing spots). The Large White is also a more handsome creature, with clear white forewings, a greenish-yellow underside to the hindwing and an impressive wingspan. Although some texts describe the Silver-washed Fritillary as Ireland's largest butterfly an occasional female Large White is bigger. However, there is some variation in size in this species, with quite diminutive Large Whites common in years when larvae find insufficient food before pupation. First generation Large Whites also have paler wingtips than those of the second generation. Its habitat and food preferences are similar to the Small White. It is not a fast flyer, unless attacked, (it then adopts an erratic and jagged flight pattern) does not appear to be a powerful flyer and yet it has been known to migrate across the seas.

It is double-brooded, appearing in May and in August/September. The second generation is far more abundant than the early brood. It is also more conspicuous because the autumn females enter gardens in search of its larval foodplant, the Cabbage (*Brassica oleracea*). It is found in a range of habitats along the coasts, in suburbs, cities, country gardens, woodland clearings and anywhere it can find nectar and larval foodplants.

It differs from the Small White in some significant respects. The female lays several eggs together, often on the underside of a leaf. When these bottle-shaped eggs hatch the larvae feed openly on the leaf. The caterpillars have no camouflage; in fact, their black, white and yellow colouration brashly advertises their presence. This indicates that the larvae are distasteful to birds, which always avoid eating them. The larvae feed ravenously, releasing unpleasant fumes from cabbage leaves which is a further deterrent. The vegetable grower often notices their presence and swiftly exterminates the caterpillars. Eggs are laid in the caterpillars by Apanteles wasps that infect many caterpillars and vast numbers are killed by these parasites. Rather cruelly, these parasites usually wait until the victim is about to pupate and has located a suitable surface on which to form a chrysalis. The yellow grubs then bite their way out and wriggle out through the hole bitten in the caterpillar's skin. They pupate beside the doomed, flabby body of the host caterpillar. The successful pupae overwinter and emerge the following May.

The Large White is distributed throughout Ireland but it is usually absent from high mountains and wetlands.

Female Large White (second brood) on Common Knapweed

Small White Bánóg Bheag
(Pieris rapae)

Small Whites mating - male above, female below

This butterfly with a wingspan c.50mm is similar to the Orange-tip and Green-veined White in size but lacks their beauty and charm. It is a plain insect with milky-white upperwing surfaces while the underside of the hindwing has a yellowish tinge. The sexes are easily distinguished by counting the spots on the upper surface of the forewings; the males have one, the females have two. The adults frequently bask on vegetation with their wings held open at an angle. It has two broods, one in May, the second in August/September. The second brood which has darker black markings is much more numerous than the first. This is probably because the overwintering pupa has a lengthy hibernation period, from about late September to May, and a large number are discovered and eaten by predators, especially by birds. It is widespread and is found in a range of habitats from coastal dunes to gardens, although it is rare or absent from wetland habitats, especially from bogs. It is also a migrant and can be seen arriving over the Irish Sea in July. This doubtless increases the numbers found in the second brood.

The males are more active than the females but both sexes can be seen taking nectar in gardens. The Small White likes Buddleia and lavenders but is not fussy about nectar sources. When a male locates a virgin female he flutters around her and she speedily succumbs, bending her abdomen to meet his. Mated females reject males by raising the abdomen to an angle of about 90 degrees.

Ovipositing females are highly conspicuous and flutter delicately over larval foodplants, touching the leaves with outstretched legs as they flutter by. Suitable leaves receive a single yellow, bottle-shaped egg. Eggs are usually laid on the underside of leaves. A very wide range of larval plants is used. The most famous is Cabbage but Charlock (*Sinapis arvensis*) on rough disturbed ground, Garden Nasturtium (*Tropaeoleum majus*) in gardens and Sea Rocket (*Cakile maritima*) at the coast are ready choices. Turnip leaves are also a favourite. The egg stage lasts about a week.

The solitary green caterpillar blends in well and is hard for the gardener to find. The caterpillar often insinuates itself into the heart of a cabbage so the gardener is unaware of the damage until it is done. Parasitic wasps certainly reduce their numbers but enough survive to pupate. Pupation takes place on the undersides of pier caps, window sills, glazing bars and on dashed walls. Despite the fact that many pupae match the surface on which they are formed (there are two colour forms, light brown and dark green) many fall victim to predation. Many caterpillars with parasitic wasp larvae inside them are killed by the parasite before pupation but some infected larvae do pupate. These never become butterflies.

This butterfly can be found throughout Ireland but numbers vary considerably from year to year.

FAMILY - PIERIDAE
Green-veined White Bánóg Uaine
(Pieris napi)

Green-veined Whites mating

First generation male Green-veined White on Common Dandelion

This species is similar in size to the Small White and at first glance it can be mistaken for it. A closer inspection reveals a butterfly whose wing veins are picked out in dark lines. The ground colour of the uppersides is milky white but some very yellow specimens are seen, especially in the second brood, from July to September. The undersides have a pale yellow hindwing and a pale yellow forewing tip. Females have two black spots on each forewing while males have one. Females also show more prominent veining than males. The first brood flies in spring and early summer, usually emerging in late April/early May while the second brood, which has clearer black markings, can be seen from July to September. This insect has a gentle, peaceful flight, especially in the cooler air temperatures of April and May. It likes wet meadows but is certainly not limited to wetland areas. Its range of larval foodplants is large but it particularly favours Watercress, Garlic Mustard (*Alliaria petiolata*) and Cuckoo Flower.

Mating pairs can often be seen on well-vegetated damp hedge banks in April/May, July/August. One frequently sees females reject male suitors by folding their wings flat against a leaf and holding her abdomen at a 90-degree angle, precisely the same tactic adopted by mated Small and Large White females. However, receptive females usually take flight but quickly land and are seduced by a scent from the male's forewings. This is a remarkably strong, sweet, fresh lemon smell and can be clearly detected by touching a captured male's forewing lightly and sniffing your fingers. What we appreciate as a lovely fragrance is clearly overpowering to the female who rapidly folds her wings and mates. A short nuptial flight follows before the pair settles on vegetation.

Both sexes nectar on a range of flowers and are frequent garden visitors. Like the Wood Whites, male Green-veined Whites engage in 'puddling' – drinking dissolved salts at the edge of water puddles in hot weather. A party of eleven males 'puddling' on a damp patch of peat in a clearing in bog woodland was observed during hot weather. Such an activity on the part of males is particularly beneficial to egg laying females who are able to prospect for suitable larval foodplants without being harassed by amorous males. Females lay on the same foodplants as the Orange-tip but choose different parts of the foodplant and often different growth forms, often choosing very small foodplants. Females flutter gently over foodplants testing their quality. Some very small seedlings are oviposited on, especially seedlings growing on soil or peat disturbed by machinery. The egg is laid on a leaf, never on a seedpod. The bottle-shaped pale yellow egg produces a green caterpillar, which closely resembles the Small White's larva. The pupa also resembles the Small White's. The chrysalis is the over-wintering stage.

This butterfly is widespread throughout Ireland although the Meadow Brown is probably more numerous.

Orange-tip Barr Buí
(*Anthocharis cardamines* subspecies *hibernica*)

Male Orange-tip

This lovely butterfly (wingspan 40-50mm, largest in the female) is on the wing between April and June. Like most species males emerge before females and are by far the more active and conspicuous. The combination of startling white and bright orange is very eye-catching and is all the more arresting due to the male's patrolling habits. The male patrols back and forth along the bright side of a hedgerow or a woodland edge. The male characteristically flies about 1 metre above ground and flies monotonously back and forth as though under very specific orders. He pauses and turns if he thinks he has seen a female. The female lacks the conspicuous orange but has a broader black tip on the forewings the edges of which are often marked with yellow. The reason the Irish Orange-tip is regarded as a subspecies is that the upperside of the female's hindwing is suffused with yellow. Both sexes have a mottled underside to the hindwing. This is primarily a butterfly of damp flowery habitats such as wet meadows, vegetated cutaway bogs, hedge banks, damp woodland clearings and riverbanks but it will breed in parks and gardens if foodplants are present in sunny situations. Its principal nectar source is Cuckoo Flower. This is its main larval foodplant but Garlic Mustard is also used. In gardens Dame's Violet (*Hesperis matronalis*) is used.

After mating, females lay their conspicuous orange bottle-shaped eggs on tall plants growing in full sun. Tall vigorous plants on the shaded side of a hedge will contain no eggs. Orange-tip eggs are so conspicuous they are visible from a distance of 1.3m or more. Eggs are usually laid singly with one egg per flower head. Although females reject flower heads containing an egg, 2-3 eggs will often be found on the same flower head. It appears that females sometimes fail to detect that a flower already has an egg. This is important because the larvae are cannibalistic.

On hatching about one week after the egg is laid the caterpillar destroys any unhatched eggs, as there must be sufficient food on each flower head. Flower pods only are consumed initially. At this early stage the larva is beige with black stubble. A large plant may contain several larvae, one on each flower head. No trouble will result as long as they do not meet. When it grows larger it becomes green with frosty flanks and is almost hairless. The caterpillar lies along the seed pod and eats it from the tip. Aligning itself in this way is presumably intended as camouflage. When about one to two weeks old the caterpillar descends halfway, or further, down the plant and commences feeding on leaves, even when flower pods are still available. Despite its matching colouration caterpillars are noticeable with their striking icy sides. By the time the larvae are fully grown (at about 32mm) the plant may be completely stripped of both leaves and seed pods. Stalks are then eaten from the top down. At this stage fully-grown larvae may meet. They react aggressively towards each other using violent head jerks. Even at this stage larvae bite each other on the back but no sustained attack or death results. When fully grown in about mid-June, caterpillars attach themselves to stalks of vegetation by two silken threads, affixed between false and true legs on both sides of the body, and by a silken pad attaching anal claspers directly to the stalk.

Male Orange-tip feeding on Ragged Robin

Larvae pupate two days later. Typically the pupa forms by a split occurring behind the head and the larval skin 'wiggles' down the body. When the skin has reached the abdomen the pupa manages to eject the spent larval skin without detaching itself from the silken pad. The pupa is fresh green with a nebulous white band along the abdomen. The thorax is sharply pointed, as is the antennae case. Unusually, for a Pierid, it sometimes pupates head down. The pupa hibernates and the adults emerge any time from about the 5th April to the end of May. Not all pupae result in adults in year one; some pupae over-winter a second year. This is probably a mechanism to guard against a very cold spring, which could result in breeding failure. In one study the ratio of pupae that result in adults after the first over-wintering is 6:1 but more study is needed to confirm this.

The Orange-tip is distributed throughout Ireland.

Female Orange-tip

Male Orange-tip (showing underside) feeding on Lady's Smock

Green Hairstreak Stiallach Uaine
(Callophrys rubi)

Green Hairstreak on bramble

The Green Hairstreak is a tiny (c.33mm wingspan) active inhabitant of bogs, bog margins, cut-away areas and woodland rides. This butterfly is on the wing in April and some survive well into July. It has been recorded as late as the 9th August in 2007. It is a well-named insect as both sexes have green undersides with a white 'hairstreak', running from the underside of the forewing to the base of the hindwing. The upper surfaces of the wings are brown and rarely seen because the species always rests with folded wings. It regulates its body temperature by constantly aligning its position in relation to the sunlight, angling its body to warm up or cool down, depending on its requirements.

The Green Hairstreak is virtually always associated with shrubs, scrub or small, often stunted trees. These are used for shelter or as vantage points and in the case of gorse, as a foodplant. A range of larval foodplants is chosen. The range includes Bilberry (*Vaccinium myrtillus*), Broom (*Cytisus scorparius*), Bird's-foot-trefoil, Tufted Vetch and blackberry. Common nectar sources for the adults include buttercups and vetches.

The behaviour of the adult varies with the time of day. In the morning adults can be seen nectaring as long as the sun is shining. After about midday the main activity seems to be perching high up on scrub/trees, guarding territories, pursuing females or chasing away other males. Territories seem to centre on a favoured leaf on a shrub; nectaring areas seem not to be occupied as territory. The butterfly is well camouflaged on fresh green spring/early summer

Green Hairstreak on Black Medic

leaves but is easily disturbed by the appearance of another butterfly (including other butterfly species). It darts out and vigorously buffets it away. Mission accomplished it promptly returns to its original leaf, alert and ready to spring on its next target. Sometimes an invading male is not so easily vanquished. A battle follows with both circling the other in a tight circle, ascending while they do so. Eventually, one accepts defeat and departs. Sometimes a female is found and several males pursue her. If she lands on a leaf the males will circle around her. Copulation in this species probably occurs high up in the shrubbery.

Females lay on the newest, most tender growing tips of gorse. The greenish-yellow, woodlouse-shaped caterpillar is extremely well hidden. When fully grown in August the larvae pupate on or under the soil.

It occurs throughout Ireland although it is much scarcer in the dry southeast with just one site at Forth Mountain in County Wexford. The distribution of this butterfly is probably under-recorded possibly because it is small and easily overlooked. It is probably most common in the southwest but any warm scrubby bog margin is worth searching.

Brown Hairstreak Stiallach Donn
(Thecla betulae)

Female Brown Hairstreak

Few people have seen this elegant butterfly. Males and females can be distinguished by the size and colour of the upper surfaces of the wings. Males have a wingspan of 38mm and the female 42mm. Both sexes have orange tails on hindwings. The upper surfaces are dark brown but the female has a striking orange band on the forewings, which is lacking in the male. Undersides are a rich orange with white streaks. In Ireland it is a butterfly of wild, unclipped hedgerows and scattered scrub on or near limestone pavement. The larval foodplant is Blackthorn (*Prunus spinosa*). It is our largest Hairstreak and a brisk flyer but it is not as hard to follow on the wing as the Green Hairstreak. At first glance the female can be mistaken, when on the wing, for a Hedge Brown (*Pyronia tithonus*). When settled, usually on a low shrub, its identity becomes immediately obvious. Females often bask with open wings on leaves of Hawthorn, Blackthorn and Hazel and will nectar on bramble and Marjoram. Males are seen much less frequently and tend to remain at the tops of Hazel. This single-brooded butterfly flies from late July to the end of September. The freshly emerged butterfly is very handsome with a silky glow on its wing surfaces. When females embark on egg laying their pristine condition is lost and very ragged butterflies can be found in late August and September.

Females crawl along the slim twigs of young Blackthorn and lay a single egg, usually in a fork but sometimes at the base of a spine. The egg is laid on the top few centimetres of the plant. The egg is white and disc-shaped and can be found during the winter on the dark twigs. Eggs hatch in April and the hairy, pale green larva feeds by nibbling at the edge of newly unfurled Blackthorn leaves. When two weeks old it eats the leaf from the mid-rib to the edge.

Female Brown Hairstreak on Blackthorn

Yellow dorsal, lateral and diagonal stripes are evident at this stage and the caterpillar is woodlouse-shaped. The black head is hidden under its prothorax except when moving or feeding. It grows slowly initially, reaching 5mm after two weeks. It rests on the underside of the leaf to which it remains attached by means of a silken thread spun with remarkable speed. Otherwise the larva is slow moving. The caterpillar feeds by day and night. The mature larva measures 17mm and turns purplish-brown at this stage. It remains stationary on the underside of a leaf for a day and then abandons the foodplant to seek a pupation site in a crevice in the soil. It pupates six days after completing its feeding. The larval stage recorded in captivity lasted forty-six days and is recorded at between forty and sixty days in the literature. The caterpillar forms a speckled brown, blunt-ended pupa. One fascinating feature of the pupa is the 'song' it produces if disturbed. The sound is audible if the pupa placed near the ear and consists of a persistent low-pitched 'Rattle Snake' rattle interspersed with a sharp chatter or crunch. This may be intended to communicate with ants in whose nests the pupa is often (or always?) formed. The chrysalis stage lasts about twenty-one days.

This butterfly is found in Counties Clare, Galway and Tipperary. It is very common in certain parts of the Burren (exceptionally abundant at Tulla townland, County Clare, along a track running east to west at M376 023) in August and early September. The absence of tall trees in the Burren, County Clare and south County Galway helps to make the butterfly more obvious because where mature, well-developed woodland exists in its habitats in Britain males stay out of sight for almost their entire lives.

Brown Hairstreak larva on Blackthorn

Brown Hairstreak pupa

Purple Hairstreak Stiallach Corcra
(Quercusia quercus)

Female Purple Hairstreak on oak

This rare butterfly is seldom seen in Ireland due to its arboreal lifestyle and the shortage of oak woods. Both sexes are similar in size with males having a wingspan of 39mm and females 37mm. The male's purple sheen covers all upper surfaces except for a black margin, while the female has a reduced, but always evident purple sheen at the base of the forewings. It is on the wing from late July to early September and over-winters in the egg stage.

It may be more common than realised because of its treetop habitat. It is possible to stand under a mature oak tree (*Quercus robur* or *Quercus petraea*), which harbours dozens of Purple Hairstreaks and not know they are present. Occasionally, in very hot weather, an individual descends to find nectar or honeydew probably due to a shortage of aphid honeydew on the canopy. When one descends it is extremely approachable; you can pull down the spray of leaves on which it is perched to get a closer view without the insect taking flight. Purple Hairstreaks will also descend close to the ground in woodland clearings in dry weather to drink from dew-spangled bramble leaves especially in the mornings, between 9am to 10.30am. Usually it is seen as a tiny silvery speck fluttering just above a spray of oak, Ash or Sweet Chestnut (*Castanea sativa*) leaves 12 metres above the ground. It is partial to nectar from Sweet Chestnut flowers.

Eggs are laid at the base of oak buds and hatch the following April when leaf burst is taking place. The larvae burrow into unfurling buds to feed. Pupation is on or below the soil. Like the Green and Brown Hairstreaks, it is quite likely that ants, which find the pupa attractive due to a 'singing' sound, care for the pupa. The pupa lasts about a month.

Male Purple Hairstreak taking water from a bramble leaf

This butterfly is recorded mainly in coastal oak woods but this probably reflects recorder activity. It is found throughout most of England where oak woods are more common and extensive colonies in England are even found on single oak trees. It is therefore possible that increased planting of oak trees in Ireland would lead to an expansion of its range. It is currently recorded in Counties Dublin, Wicklow, Waterford, Cork, Kerry, Clare, Galway, Roscommon, Mayo, Sligo and Fermanagh.

Small Copper Copróg Bheag
(Lycaena phlaeas)

Male Small Copper on Ox-eye Daisy

This copper-coloured butterfly is extremely active in hot weather. It is found in coastal dunes, wet meadows, woodland rides, clearings, bog margins, cut-away areas and even gardens. The colour variant Small Copper with blue spots on the hindwings, known as *caeruleopunctata,* can be quite common. Although small (only 32-35 mm across wings) the male is highly evident due to its habit of darting from its resting place, pursuing another butterfly to eject it from the territory before returning to its vantage point. This butterfly enjoys nectaring on a wide range of flowers such as Cuckoo Flower, Ox-eye Daisy, Common Knapweed, heathers (*Erica* ssp) and Fleabane. It is also fond of basking on bare patches of ground. Its main foodplant is Common Sorrel (*Rumex acetosa*) but it also uses Broad-leaved Dock (*Rumex obtusifolius*). The main flight periods are May and July-August.

The female lays her white disc-shaped egg singly on the underside of the leaf of the foodplant and a week later the tiny green slug-like larva emerges and feeds on the underside of the leaf. Feeding damage is quite diagnostic of its presence as it leaves the top layer of the leaf intact, giving it a transparent appearance. The larva pupates, as far as is known, low down in vegetation or on the ground. The pupa, which is rounded and brownish-yellow, lasts about two weeks but will last longer when the larvae have over-wintered.

Caeruleopunctata form

This butterfly is widespread in Ireland but is usually seen in ones and twos. However, sometimes large numbers are seen. Thirty were observed on one occasion, all nectaring in a small wildflower meadow that was surrounded by hedgerows. It also tolerates windswept locations as long as its main foodplant, Common Sorrel is present. It can no longer be considered a general countryside insect as many farms have eliminated all wild flowers and sorrels needed for it to exist.

Small Blue Gormán Beag
(Cupido minimus)

Male Small Blue

This tiny butterfly has a wingspan of 16 to 25mm. Its undersides are grey and uppersides smoky brown. The male is distinguished from the female by a faint dusting of blue scales at the bases of the upper surfaces of its forewings and hindwings. When perched this dusting is barely perceptible but in flight the males look more 'blue' than you would expect having seen the perched individual. It is usually seen feeding on Bird's-foot-trefoil and Kidney Vetch (*Anthyllis vulneraria*), which is also the larval foodplant. It can be seen on the wing from the second half of May to the first half of June, after which it becomes scarcer. It hibernates as a fully fed larva.

The larval foodplant cannot withstand competition from vigorous grasses and therefore it is usually found on coastal dunes, dry coastal grasslands, quarries (inland and coastal) and calcareous grassland that is grazed or windswept. The butterfly itself is found in these habitats where it prefers to keep to sunny, sheltered slopes within these areas. Thus it is found in the dry coastal calcareous grassland of the Ballyryan district in the west of the Burren. Here it is found in small, sheltered hollows with a scattering of Bracken (*Pteridium aquilinum*).

The male's flight is very difficult to follow if disturbed or pursuing another Small Blue. But if you remain very still it usually returns to its original perching spot. It is a sedentary butterfly and rarely moves far. Certainly colonies breeding on linear coastal dune systems bear witness to this phenomenon. Butterflies almost never venture beyond the shelter of the sand dunes. They are therefore very vulnerable to local extinction due to local habitat destruction.

Mature Small Blue larva on Kidney Vetch in late July

The female is easily observed while laying eggs on Kidney Vetch flowers. A single disc-shaped white egg is laid in each inflorescence and is easy to see, despite its small size. The egg results in a tiny woodlouse-shaped larva after two weeks.

The caterpillar feeds on the contents of each floret. It shares the pale, greyish-brown hue of the spent flowers and so is well concealed. By late July the Kidney Vetch flower heads are beginning disintegrate and the fully fed larva departs to hibernate just below ground for a ten-month period. It then pupates forming a pupa similar in colour to the larvae. The pupa lasts two weeks.

The distribution of the Small Blue is chiefly coastal in Ireland, but there are inland records for Counties Tipperary, Clare, Galway and Roscommon. It has disappeared from Northern Ireland, but is found in County Donegal. It is probably overlooked in inland areas but it is more vulnerable inland as eskers are often destroyed for gravel extraction or undergo successional changes with woodland eventually overwhelming grassland flora. A careful watch needs to be kept on its coastal habitats however as golf links often result in re-seeding large areas with a Perennial Rye-grass or fescue monoculture.

Common Blue Gormán Coiteann
(Polyommatus icarus/
Polyommatus icarus subspecies mariscolore)

Male Common Blue on Bird's-foot-trefoil

This is a stunning blue butterfly (wingspan 29-38mm) which usually emerges in late May. Its first brood is on the wing until the end of June. The second brood flies from early August and it may be found even into early October. It hibernates in the larval stage.

The Common Blue is especially common on poor, well-drained sandy soils, such as sand dunes, and rocky outcrops, such as in the Burren. It is also found on heavier, wetter soils where Bird's–foot-trefoil straggles over taller vegetation. Well-grazed fields with Bird's-foot-trefoil will also have Common Blues but at a lower density. They are also found in woodland clearings.

A form of the female Common Blue known as *mariscolore* occurs in Ireland and this is blue with orange spots on the upper surface of the forewings and hindwings. In England the brown-winged females are the norm but these can also be found here. A form of the female, which looks to be an intermediate form between the British and Irish forms also occurs here. This has brown upperwings with a strong dusting of blue scales. The male Common Blue is larger and a brighter blue than those found in Britain but smaller specimens do occur here.

Female Common Blue Mariscolore form on Bird's-foot-trefoil

Females are less obvious and less active than males which fly ponderously yet purposefully over Bird's-foot-trefoil to seek a female. Although territorial, males are not as possessive of their patch as the Green Hairstreak or Small Copper. Common Blues will chase other males but lose interest quite quickly, so that it appears that males are only approaching other males to determine whether they are in fact females or not. When the sexes are joined in copulation the male carries the female on a short nuptial flight.

Females start to lay their eggs about two days after mating. Eggs are pale green at first, but later turn white. The eggs are disc-shaped. Eggs are laid in a curious manner. The female walks over the trefoil leaves and flowers 'drumming' with her front legs and bending her antennae to taste and smell the foodplant ascertaining its suitability. She often tests the leaves with her proboscis (tongue). When she is satisfied with the quality of the plant, egg laying follows. She curves her abdomen to make contact with the upper or underside of the leaves, stalks and flowers of Bird's-foot-trefoil and even blades of grass. The egg is deposited very carefully. It takes her longer to lay her egg than other species that lay their eggs singly (such as the Small White). The female Common Blue punctuates her egg laying with nectaring on flowers such as Bird's-foot-trefoil and Common Dandelion. Females become tattered during egg laying.

The eggs hatch after about nine days. The larva is very small and even after a week of feeding it is still extremely diminutive. It is light green and its most obvious feature at this stage is its black head. It is slug-like in appearance. The caterpillar eats the leaves of its foodplant by stripping the top layer of the leaf but leaving the basic leaf structure intact. Feeding damage appears as a pale grey half-moon in an otherwise lush leaf. By early July the larva has doubled in size to 4mm and by mid-July it reaches about 11mm in length and 4mm in width. The larvae are now green with a thin yellow stripe evident from the second or third segment onwards (i.e. from head to tail end). A deep green dorsal line is also evident. At this stage the caterpillar is now reducing the leaf to shreds. The larvae studied in captivity pupated simultaneously in late July. The pupae are olive green and rounded at both ends. They range in size from 8-9mm but the most apparent difference between the male and female pupa lies in the width that ranges from 3mm in the female to 5mm in the male. The male emerged on 3rd August – a pupal stage lasting thirteen days. The female emerged a day later. The female recorded was bred from a pair from Bull Island, County Dublin and was of English/Welsh coloration with chocolate-brown wings and orange half-moons around the edges. The adult female was also small like her counterpart across the Irish Sea. Interestingly, her mother was of the typical Irish *mariscolore* form.

The Common Blue is well distributed throughout Ireland and is especially abundant in coastal regions.

FAMILY - LYCAENIDAE
Holly Blue Gormán Cuilinn
(Celastrina argiolus)

Male Holly Blue on bramble

This is a striking butterfly (with a wingspan of about 35mm) when seen with wings open or when fluttering around Holly, Ivy or bramble in bright sunlight. Both sexes are a bright lilac blue but can be distinguished by the fact that the female has more pronounced black tips on the upperside of the forewings. The summer generation females have more extensive black tips than the first generation. It is typically seen in at least two and indeed even in three generations a year. The tendency to produce multiple broods increases with latitude. Three broods have been recorded in County Cork with two in County Kildare and only one full brood in County Down. The adult can be seen from late March/April - early June, early July – early September, and sometimes in late September/October.

Summer generation female

Spring generation female

It is primarily a butterfly of hedgerows, woodland edges and mature gardens, even in built up areas. It nectars on hedgerow plants, especially on blackberry blooms and aphid honeydew which coats the leaves of trees in summer. It is an unusual butterfly: in some years it is very common and in other years it is quite scarce. This does not appear to be linked to the weather and may be caused by the predation levels attributed to ichneumon wasps. It has different larval foodplants depending on the time of year: it primarily uses female Holly in spring and Ivy in summer. It is also very tame, especially when egg laying or puddling. Otherwise they can be quite elusive, usually seen fluttering around treetops or with males chasing each other. The moment the sun stops shining Holly Blue seem to vanish. Mating takes place on a shrub, typically using a bramble leaf as a platform. No courtship ritual takes place; the male simply lands beside the female and if she is receptive, pairing immediately follows. A copulation observed lasted one hour twenty-three minutes. Adult females can be seen laying on Holly flowers or on very young berries in late April/May. White disc-shaped eggs are laid on the underside of the flower or berry. These later turn white. A Holly growing in a warm, sunny, sheltered location will be especially favoured and females are irresistibly drawn to them.

Holly Blues mating

The egg hatches after a week and the tiny, green, slug-like larva clings to the underside of the tender young berry. It bites a hole in it and enlarges this. It feeds in this way throughout its life. Larvae have been observed feeding on tender new Holly leaves especially on plants with few berries. Leaves are eaten from the centre and edge with the lower layer of the leaf stripped, creating a translucent appearance. Larvae are occasionally found on male Holly, feeding on leaves. Fully grown larvae measure 12-13mm and some mature larvae sport a maroon dorsal stripe and a pinkish tinge. When fully grown larvae desert the foodplant and despite thorough searches of the foodplant and surrounding vegetation, no sign of the larvae or brown pupae will be found. Thus it is most likely that they pupate away from the foodplant on the ground. The final generation, which breeds on mature flowering Ivy, hibernates in the pupal stage. They may pupate among the Ivy since Holly Blue males, which emerge before females in March/April, scour the Ivy searching for newly emerging females.

In the past the species was chiefly known from woodlands near the coast and from the remnants of old woods, but it has certainly enjoyed an expansion in recent years and is being found in areas it was never recorded in before. It is being found far inland and away from woodland, as long as there are mature hedgerows. Since 2003 it has been noted in gardens where it had not appeared previously. This expansion has been noted throughout the country and may perhaps be a response to warmer conditions.

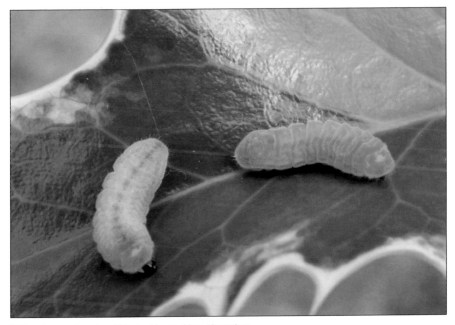

Mature larvae placed on Holly leaf to provide a clear view.

Red Admiral Aimiréal Dearg
(Vanessa atalanta)

Red Admiral on Buddleia

With its jet black and deep red forewings this large, handsome general countryside butterfly is unmistakeable Males have a wingspan of 64-72mm and females 70-78mm. It is an annual migrant that arrives from the southern Europe and North Africa chiefly in May and June but some are seen in April. Fishermen off the south County Wexford coast often find individual Red Admirals alighting on their boats, during migration in May/June. It is possible that some overwinter here successfully but the vast bulk are migrants. It may be seen on the wing until late in November. Recently the egg, larval and pupal stages were discovered in Howth, County Dublin during winter and spring. There is evidence that some Red Admirals leave Ireland in September and October and migrate south. Certainly if you stand on Portmarnock Strand,

Red Admirals mating

County Dublin or Hook Head, County Wexford in early September you will see Red Admirals flying south-eastwards over the sea.

It can turn up anywhere and spends a lot of time on nectar-rich plants, especially Buddleia. and as long as there are tall, sheltered, partly shaded Stinging Nettles they will breed in gardens. It has been suggested (*Millennium Atlas of Britain and Ireland*, page 194) that mating "occurs immediately after overwintering and migrants from north Africa and continental Europe normally arrive mated". However mating does occur in Ireland. The mating pictured below took place in late July, well after overwintering and migration. The male engages the female and both sexes flutter delicately, with the male just behind the female, flying at about 2.5m (7½feet) above the ground. The female alights on a branch or leaf and the male flutters around her. When the female decides to remain settled the male alights beside her, folds his wings and pairing occurs.

Females lay a single egg on the tip of a Stinging Nettle and quickly depart to seek another shaded plant. The larva lives alone and is protected by spinning a 'tent' around itself by fastening a young leaf around itself with silk. Two colour forms are found: one black with a yellow lateral stripe and the other green with a yellow lateral stripe with yellow markings above this running in broken lines down its length. It feeds in a succession of these 'tents.' After feeding for four weeks it spins several leaves together near the top of the foodplant and bends the stem below these leaves by chewing it. It pupates inside this shelter. The chrysalis stage lasts about eighteen days.

The Red Admiral can appear anywhere in Ireland – in cities, gardens, coasts, bogs, wooded areas, meadows-anywhere there are sources of nectar and nettles. It has a liking for tree sap, over-ripe fruit, (including blackberries) and flowering Ivy, all of which can attract it to your garden.

Red Admiral (underside) nectaring on Buddleia

Painted Lady Áilleán
(Cynthia cardui)

Painted Lady on Common Knapweed

This is an annual migrant that is extremely abundant in some years and much less so in others. Like its relative the Red Admiral it is a fast, powerful insect and while its brown, orange and white wings lack the elegance of the Red Admiral, its patterning is similar in organisation. Its size shows great variation, with individuals ranging from 58 – 70 mm in the male and 62 – 74 mm in the female. Sexes are alike in colour. Its habits and lifecycle are very similar to the Red Admiral, except that it has several foodplants: Stinging Nettle, Artichoke (*Cynara solymus*) and thistles. It seems to appear in Ireland later than the Red Admiral, becoming noticeable in May and persisting until the end of September. Although it produces a native generation of butterflies these perish when the temperatures drop. The Painted Lady is never seen in November, or early spring, while Red Admirals will be seen late and early in the year. They have no hibernation stage and continuously brood in Africa and in other hot climates. It gorges on nectar from Buddleia, Common Knapweed, Devil's-bit Scabious and Red Clover. They roost in trees and bask on these in the evening before retiring for the night. It is possible that mating takes place in trees. It is a wary insect and does not usually allow a close approach except in cool weather.

The egg laying, larval and chrysalis stages are very similar to the Red Admiral's life cycle, except that the stages can happen within a month during hot weather. The larva is spiny and black with a single yellow lateral stripe. The chrysalis, like that of the Peacock and Small Tortoiseshell, occurs in two colour forms. One is a pale metallic grey and the other is grey/brown and suffused with gold. The pupal stage is usually of about two weeks' duration.

The Painted Lady is distributed throughout Ireland and can appear anywhere there are flowers.

FAMILY - NYMPHALIDAE
Small Tortoiseshell Ruán Beag
(Aglais urticae)

Small Tortoiseshell (first brood) on Creeping Thistle

The Small Tortoiseshell (wingspan 50-56mm, sexes identical in colour) is one of Ireland's most widely distributed butterflies but its abundance varies from year to year. There are usually two generations a year. It is on the wing until May and occasionally up to early June, in a cool spring. These adults produce eggs in April and May that result in a short-lived generation that is on the wing in July. These mid-summer adults produce a long-lived generation which emerge late in August and hibernate from October to March. However there is considerable variation and Small Tortoiseshell larvae have been found in late September and even early October. This suggests a third generation occurs during years with prolonged good weather. Adults can be seen on the wing as early as 1st February but later in March is more usual.

The adults that emerge from hibernation are extremely fast, vigilant, wide-ranging insects and are difficult to approach closely. They feed on Common Dandelion, the most commonly used nectar this early in the year. Small Tortoiseshells also enjoy Grape Hyacinth. In wetland areas the butterfly nectars from Goat Willow catkins (*Salix caprea*). From March-June the priority of Small Tortoiseshells is to seek a mate and lay eggs. The main activity of late summer adults is to feed up for the long hibernation period and Buddleia, hebe, Ice Plant, Michelmas Daisy in gardens and Devil's-bit Scabious, Common Knapweed and thistles in the wild are much sought after. Sap bleeding from damaged deciduous trees is also exploited.

One of the reasons Small Tortoiseshells are so familiar and beloved of the general public is because of their bright colours, chiefly bright orange, black and yellow, with bluish shells decorating the wing edges and its tendency to stay close to our gardens and homes. It frequently enters houses in late summer, prospecting for a hibernation site and will spend cool nights in September indoors, exiting through open windows when the heat of good September weather rouses the butterfly. Eventually it will settle in curtain folds in houses or in sheds for the winter. It can also be found in disused chimneybreasts, air vents and cavities in old stone-built walls.

On emergence from hibernation it quickly seeks to reproduce. Males and females gather at Stinging Nettle beds from late March up to end of May or even early June. In early March nettles are still very young. Males quarter low over the nettles ranging widely over the field battling against other males with each trying to fly above the other. This is one way of distinguishing the sexes that look identical. Eventually one male peels away from the battle to resume his search for a female. When he spots one a high-speed chase ensues and if already mated, she tries to evade the pursuing male and is often assisted in this evasion by another male. She often flies into the flight path of another male and the second male gives chase. In the subsequent confusion the female changes direction sharply and vanishes. If she is willing, she leads the male in a merry dance, testing his staying power. If he manages to keep her in his sights, mating follows in a tussock of dense grass or a nettle patch.

Females lay on young, non-flowering nettles growing on the sunny edge of the nettle patch. Eggs are laid in a large batch on the underside of a nettle leaf near the very top of a plant. The green eggs are very similar in colour to the leaf. They are laid in batches of dozens of layers piled on top of layers. Females have been observed dying immediately after laying while males remain active.

Larvae hatch after about ten days and spin a web over the top of the nettle patch, feeding colonially. When the leaves are reduced to a skeletal state the entire colony migrates to the next nettle top. Sometimes a group of caterpillars gets left behind but these soon catch up and seem to know where the rest of their colony is. The colony is probably located by scent. When young, the larvae are an indeterminate grey colour and lack the conspicuous black and yellow warning coloration they acquire later - a colour scheme that serves as a warning to birds that the larvae are distasteful. Even at this young stage they do possess a defence; if disturbed or seized they collectively emit a foul smelling green liquid from their mouthparts. After five or six days (post-moult) larvae spin a web over larger, more mature leaves. When about eleven days old, caterpillars feed openly in small groups without spinning webs. At this stage they are about 15mm in length and the yellow and black patterning is evident.

Larvae continue to move from one nettle to another, leaving the previous nettle's top quarter of its leaves reduced to shreds. Leaves are eaten from the centre and edge. Some desert the colony and move with brisk determination to search for the next vigorous nettle with tender growing tips. Typically however caterpillars feed in groups of three to five when older. At about eighteen days old the first individuals begin prospecting for pupation sites. When searching for a safe place to form its chrysalis, larvae are swift and purposeful, scaling large objects, like walls, in their search. Some pupate under nettle leaves or even on fabric.

Small Tortoiseshell caterpillar on nettle   Small Tortoiseshell chrysalis on carpet fabric

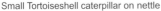

Interestingly, pupae vary in colour according to where the caterpillar pupated. Caterpillars from the same colony can produce different coloured chrysalises. Larvae that pupate on dark coloured surfaces produce a dark brownish-grey chrysalis, while those formed on brighter surfaces result in a light coloured greenish-gold pupa with a metallic sheen. Like other members of the Vanessids, the chrysalis is attached to a surface by its abdomen only. Larvae that pupate on surfaces that are neither light nor dark produce a pupa that is light beige in hue with some metallic gold speckles on the spikes on its abdomen and thoracic points. This shows an ability to adopt a shade to blend in with its surroundings. The pupa itself is about 21mm long.

About twelve days after pupation the wing colour and patterning of the butterfly is clearly visible through the wing cases of the pupa. The adult emerges at twelve days and crawls up a plant stem, remaining stationary while its crumpled wings unfold. On emergence the butterflies feed on thistles and remain close to the breeding ground instead of wandering. They behave much like their parents did in spring.

Small Tortoiseshells are fortunate in one important respect that accounts for their being very abundant and widespread. In sheep farming areas all of the grassland vegetation is grazed severely, including wild flowers. Two notable plants sheep avoid are Stinging Nettles, the larval foodplant and thistles, the adult butterfly's chief nectar source in these areas. However a sharp decline in the Small Tortoiseshell is reported from southeast England and this is possibly the result of a parasitic fly (*Sturmia bella*) that is new to Britain. The continued abundance of one of our most common butterflies cannot be taken for granted.

Peacock Péacóg
(Inachis io)

Peacock on Common Knapweed

This is one of our most beautiful butterflies. By contrast with its glorious uppersides, its underwings are sombre black, but with an intricate lace pattern. Although the Peacock is a butterfly of the general countryside it breeds chiefly near wooded areas. It is large and powerful and the sexes are alike except that females are noticeably larger (63 mm wingspan in the male, up to 70 mm in the female). It likes woodland edges, rides and clearings, and feeds for long periods on nectar, especially in late summer and autumn. It is single-brooded and long-lived and is in the adult stage at all times of the year, except for the end of June and most of July. It has been seen as late as the 22nd June. By this stage it is about eleven months old, a long life for a winged insect.

Huge populations often develop during August and early September in flower-rich meadows and bogs along woodland edges. These adults are quite approachable as they gorge on the nectar of Common Knapweed, Field Scabious, Devil's-bit Scabious, Buddleia and heathers (*Erica* ssp).

Peacocks hibernate early, with many disappearing by mid-September. They hibernate irrespective of how pleasant the September weather is. Peacocks choose woods, sheds and hollow trees, but avoid entering houses. Large numbers may congregate together and dozens were discovered hibernating beneath a large bog oak trunk. When disturbed, hibernating Peacocks flash their large eye-spots and make a snake-like hissing by rubbing their forewings against their hindwings. Several individuals do this in unison; the effect is to terrify a small bird into the belief that a predator has been encountered.

Despite the camouflage derived from their undersides, and impressive impersonations, large numbers must fail to survive the winter: one can return in March/April to an area which held hundreds the previous August and find less than half a dozen. The lowness of the numbers is partly explained by the fact that post-hibernation males are territorial. In spring, Peacocks are extremely alert, wary and difficult to approach. They spend a lot of their time basking on bare ground. The important business at hand now is to mate. Like Small Tortoiseshells, male Peacocks establish territories and investigate any butterfly or small bird in the hope of finding a mate. Females make the males work hard for the right to mate – just like their relative the Small Tortoiseshell.

Peacock larvae feeding (top of leaf) and basking

Stinging Nettle is the larval foodplant and like the Small Tortoiseshell a large number of green eggs are laid in a batch beneath a leaf near the top of the plant. However, unlike the Small Tortoiseshell the Peacock always chooses taller plants to lay its eggs on. They are always part of a large clump and in a sunny place, usually sheltered by scrub/trees. The larvae which live colonially within webs, are chiefly black with white speckles and prominent spines. When larger they feed outside the webs, initially in smaller groups, later alone. Fully-grown larvae are over 42mm long and pupate when about a month old. The pupa occurs in the same two colour forms as the Small Tortoiseshell's but it is larger, reaching 26mm in length. The chrysalis stage lasts two weeks. It is interesting to note that Peacocks in Brittany, France are bivoltine (double-brooded). Eggs that result in the second brood are laid in July. With the Irish climate warming, the Peacock may become double-brooded in Ireland. There is evidence

Eggs on underside of nettle leaf laid simultaneously by three females

this may be happening as some freshly emerged male Peacocks in early August have been observed pursuing females, behaviour inconsistent with a reproductive diapause.

The Peacock is widespread and common and often found in gardens during August. It is very fond of Buddleia and a specimen flowering mainly in August/September will be host to several of these extravagantly liveried butterflies.

Pearl-bordered Fritillary Fritileán Péarlach
(Boloria euphrosyne)

Freshly emerged Female Pearl-bordered Fritillary on Hazel

The distribution of the Pearl-bordered Fritillary is limited to the scrublands of the Burren in Counties Clare and Galway where it was discovered in 1922. The Pearl-bordered Fritillary (wingspan 44-47mm, females larger than males) appears at the very beginning of May following a warm April and lasts until early June in hot weather. Its flight period extends later into June during cooler conditions. A cold April such as that experienced in 2008 will delay the emergence until mid-May, underlining how weather dependent this butterfly is. Its wings have bright orange upper surfaces with black spots. The undersides have a beautiful patterning, featuring a string of seven silver pearls adorning the outer margin. The sexes are similar in appearance except that the female often has a paler orange margin running along the uppersides of the forewings and hindwings; the black markings on these margins are larger while the male's uppersides are a deeper orange.

The adult is on the wing from 9.30am and is active all day until about 7 o'clock in the evening provided the weather is warm and sunny. Both males and females bask to warm up and both sexes feed on Bugle (*Ajuga reptans*), buttercups and Bird's-foot-trefoil. Males are far more active and obvious because they spend much of their time patrolling back and forth over a large clearing in Hazel scrub. Males can sometimes be seen patrolling by the dozen, passing back and forth over an area, quartering low and fast over the ground. It can sometimes be mistaken for the Wall Brown but the Pearl-bordered Fritillary lands less frequently during

Male Pearl-bordered Fritillary basking on limestone pavement during cloudy interval

hot weather and their wings have no eyespots. The best time to get a close view of the Pearl-bordered Fritillary is after 8.30am on a warm morning. Adults soon emerge from grassland and vegetation near the Hazel scrub and hold their wings wide open against limestone pavement to bask and heat up. Boreens alongside scrub are also used as basking spots. Basking also occurs during overcast conditions that follow a period of sunshine and this elusive butterfly will then allow close approach.

The larval foodplant is Common Dog-violet and females seek violets that are bathed in sunshine and rise above the tangle of nearby vegetation. Bun-shaped eggs are laid singly and hatch in two weeks. Larvae are black and spiny and feed until the third moult. They hibernate until March when feeding is resumed and cease feeding in April, when pupation occurs. The duration of this stage varies with the weather and has been recorded as lasting from nine to nineteen days.

The question as to why the distribution is limited to the Burren is an interesting one. Was it introduced to the area? Why was it never recorded in historically managed woodlands, like those in Killarney? Whatever the answer it should be monitored as no other Irish butterfly has such a geographically confined distribution. Should the limestone pavement become shrouded in Hazel scrub the violets found there would become unsuitable for breeding and the butterfly would become extinct.

Pearl-bordered Fritillary habitat in the Burren

Pearl-bordered Fritillary - underside

Dark Green Fritillary Fritileán Dúghlas
(Mesoacidalia aglaia formerly Argynnis aglaja)

Male Dark Green Fritillary on Red Clover

A large, powerful, bright orange butterfly battling with the breeze on a cliff top, limestone pavement or sand dune can only be a Dark Green Fritillary. Startlingly visible yet frustratingly evasive, it is a grassland species that breeds on Common Dog-violet. Both sexes have a greenish underside on the hindwing. This area is spangled with bright silver spots that gleam and act as a mirror that reflects the vegetation the butterfly roosts in. Males, at 60-63 mm across the wings are smaller than females (69-70 mm) but in the field this is not a reliable indicator. Behaviour is more diagnostic of gender. Females spend more time perching on grassland vegetation, vibrating their wings as though shivering from cold. They also feed more frequently on the nectar of thistles, hawkbits, orchids, Red Clover and Thyme. Males are air-borne for most of the day scouring the grasslands for females. The best time to get close to a male is to visit its habitat in early morning and look for the flowers on which it feeds in preparation for its daylong search. Despite the fact that most sightings are of single airborne males, they can be observed feeding in small groups on warm mornings. On sites with high

Female Dark Green Fritillary on Thyme

Dark Green Fritillary showing hindwings with green and silver markings

populations males and females can be found in the evenings settling to roost together in tall grassland. Usually only a single male is seen but he is extremely conspicuous, surging powerfully across the grasslands. He will pursue anything that flies – one was even observed pursuing a skylark. When a male does stop to drink nectar during the heat of the day, he behaves as if in a frantic hurry, stabbing his proboscis wildly into the flower and swiftly departing. This butterfly is generally seen from late June to the middle of August, but there are records from early June.

Females lay on violets whose leaves stand proud of surrounding vegetation and also deposit several eggs in the vicinity of the foodplant. The larvae hatch about two weeks later and hibernate. The caterpillar is spiny and black with red spots along its flanks. Its brownish pupa is formed among vegetation litter and lasts about a month.

In Ireland the Dark Green Fritillary is mainly coastal in its distribution and breeds on dune systems. There are inland colonies in north County Clare breeding on limestone grassland while in west County Kildare and County Offaly it breeds on flower-rich cut-away bogs. It is often found breeding at very low densities over large areas of habitat. In highly suitable habitat in the Burren and County Donegal it occurs in large numbers. For the dramatic power of its flight, there is no other Irish butterfly to rival it.

Silver-washed Fritillary Fritileán Geal
(Argynnis paphia)

Male Silver-washed Fritillary

This is a large eye-catching inhabitant of deciduous and mixed woodland where light reaches the woodland floor. Its wingspan varies considerably, with some males being only slightly larger than a female Small Tortoiseshell. Large individuals reach 80mm. This size variation occurs within colonies. It can be seen from mid-June to early September with a peak in late July. Both males and females appear similar on the wing: both are large bright orange butterflies. Males have prominent black wing bars on the forewings while females have spots and are paler orange. Males are more prominent and emerge first; they can be seen nectaring on brambles (Rubus ssp). Males swoop rapidly over clearings and sweep up to the treetops, apparently vanishing into the canopy, only to appear moments later on a pink blackberry blossom. Males appear to be sexually immature when they first emerge – they spend a few days basking and nectaring and show no inclination to search for a mate. A Buddleia in a sunny sheltered clearing will hold a bachelor party of over a dozen males, eagerly feeding up.

This butterfly has attracted a great deal of study and observing it will show you why. It is elegant and powerful in its movements with stunning upper wings and beautifully patterned undersides, with the largely greenish hindwing suffused with pale silver streaks. It also has a fascinating life cycle. The courtship is remarkably charming, almost romantic, and can be observed in July in most deciduous woodlands where light bathes violets on the wood's floor. When a male locates a willing female a synchronised aerial courtship follows, with the female maintaining a straight flight line, while her suitor swoops below her and then loops in front of her. When she is impressed both land and the male wafts scent from his forewing's black scent bars over her. Utterly seduced, pairing occurs. The male carries the female to a tree and there they settle to mate, both resting with closed wings.

Females only become conspicuous when laying eggs and this is worth seeing. Females flutter low over the ground, locating the scent of violets, the larval foodplant. She tends to seek areas that receive good sunlight, usually near the end of a path or along a ride or woodland clearing or in open woodland. Violets near tree trunks or violets growing beneath coppiced Hazel are favoured. She then lands on a tree trunk nearby, settles and deposits at least one egg, sometimes more. Females will lay on mossy trunks of Hawthorn but oak is also used. The eggs may be laid no more than 1 metre up the trunk but are often placed considerably higher. Beech trees are never chosen for ovipositing because violets growing under them are in deep shade and the larvae require sunlight to make digestion possible.

Female Silver-washed Fritillary

The egg hatches after two weeks and after eating its eggshell, the caterpillar hibernates on the tree. It emerges in spring and begins its long journey to seek violet leaves. By early May the caterpillar is developing very quickly, moulting every six days. Moulting takes place on the underside of violet leaves. Like other Nymphalids, it is a spiny creature with yellow stripes running the length of its body. These are both dorsal and lateral. The background colour is a rich brown. The caterpillar spends much of its time basking and it is extremely difficult to see as it lies on brown leaves in bright sunshine with tiny shadows cast by wispy grass, adding to the blending ability of the caterpillar. When feeding it takes long, curved bites out of violet leaves with both tender and mature leaves eaten. It also eats young shoots, flowers, pods and seeds and roosts under the leaves. After bouts of voracious feeding it rests, often in a sleepy posture, with the head slightly to one side. Near the end of the larval stage it reduces large mature violets to a few leaves. At this stage it has reached 36mm in length. When fully grown it is about 39mm and the caterpillar abandons its foodplant and wanders with a sense of urgency. It attaches itself to the underside of a twig with silk and hangs by its anal claspers. It pupates after two days of lying in this position. It typically pupates in early June.

The chrysalis is pale brown with ten beautiful, gleaming, metallic gold markings on the thorax. The metallic gold mirrors the colour of the surroundings; if placed in a green box the gold becomes a metallic green. This is doubtless intended as camouflage to help it blend in with the changing colour of vegetation. If disturbed, it wriggles violently. The pupa is about 23mm long and darkens to a dark grey, prior to ecdysis (emergence). The pupal stage lasts about fourteen days and up to three weeks in cool conditions. The fresh adults colours have a beautiful 'velvet' glow.

This fritillary is found in scattered locations throughout Ireland, even in quite small woodlands. It can be found in upland woods, like those at Glendalough, County Wicklow, coastal woods such as The Raven, County Wexford, urban woods like the Phoenix Park, Dublin, woods on heavy soils at Tintern Abbey woods in County Wexford and even among the hazel scrub in the Burren. We are fortunate that it is so widespread because it is declining in Britain where its range has contracted to the west and south. We should be vigilant and ensure by maintaining rides and clearings, that our population does not follow suit.

Marsh Fritillary Fritileán Réisc
(Euphydryas aurinia)

Female Marsh Fritillary on Devil's-bit Scabious

This exquisite butterfly has a wingspan of about 42mm in the male, and 47mm in the female. Its wings have an intricate patterning of cream, yellow, orange and red on a black background. Sexes are alike but females are noticeably larger. It is a highly variable species and no two individuals have precisely the same patterning. It is declining alarmingly throughout Europe including Britain and Ireland and is placed on the Annex II list under the EU Habitats Directive. This requires the member governments of the EU to designate SAC's (Special Areas of Conservation) for the species. Regrettably the Irish response has not been very helpful. Part of the state's approach has been to designate the national parks as SAC's for the butterfly, a policy that proved futile when the species disappeared from Killarney National Park. To date (2008) only fourteen areas have been designated for the species. Despite requests to the government to designate important breeding sites as SAC's for the butterfly, nothing has been done. Neither is there any apparent management plan in place. Recently (2006) the butterfly was reintroduced to Killarney from a stock gathered in Kerry. However the available habitat in Killarney is small and the "colony" is probably unviable. Meanwhile a colony west of Loughrea, one of the largest in Ireland, is completely unprotected. This site is about 40 hectares in area and is one of the largest areas of suitable habitat. Yet the plea to designate this site has met with little interest.

One ray of hope lies in the surveys being conducted by the NPWS (National Parks and Wildlife Service), coordinated by the IPCC (Irish Peatland Conservation Council) to identify Marsh Fritillary breeding sites within declared SAC's. Management of these sites is vital as encroachment by trees, scrub and tall vegetation destroys the habitat of this grassland species. The Marsh Fritillary thrives on grassland that contains at least a 25% density of the larval foodplant Devil's-bit Scabious. The grassland that is favoured must have a sward of 10-15cm (4-12 inches). The grassland should also have a tussocky structure, some light cattle or horse grazing and nectar sources. Shelter provided by a landscape feature and/or scattered scrub is also a requirement of this butterfly.

The butterfly is on the wing from about mid-May to the end of June. The larval stage lasts from late July to May and the pupal stage lasts about two weeks. Adult butterflies are particularly attracted to Tormentil (*Potentilla erecta*) (a species which is characteristic of every Marsh Fritillary site), Meadow Thistle (*Cirsium dissectum*), Lady's Smock and marsh orchids.

Males are much in evidence from mid-May onwards as they fly low over their breeding area, which may be as small as a hectare or as large as 40 hectares. They bask in early morning in order to raise their body temperature to the level when they can be active. When ready they zigzag low over the grassland and in bright sunshine their flight is hard to follow. This butterfly's mobility is highly dependent on air temperature. The hotter it is, the faster the males can fly. Despite being hard to follow the butterfly frequently perches on low scrub, flowers or low vegetation and will remain very still, making it easy to observe and photograph. This habit of landing on the ground or low vegetation, especially when a cloud obscures the sun, makes the butterfly an easy victim for insect predators. Crab spiders often pounce on Marsh Fritillary butterflies that perch on the Cuckoo Flower. Marsh Fritillaries roost in grass tussocks and that also makes them very vulnerable. The result is that adults have a lifespan of only a few days.

The female emerges and crawls up a grass stalk to dry her wings. She has eggs that are simply awaiting fertilization. A male often finds her at this stage and mating follows quickly. A short nuptial flight follows and a scent may be released during the mating because other males are attracted to the pair. Her body is heavy and her flight is very slow. She barely manages to fly a few feet in cool weather. It is vital for a creature that is so short-lived to lay quickly and this she does.

The Marsh Fritillary will lay its eggs from about 11am to 6pm. She seeks out a foodplant (in Ireland it is always Devil's-bit Scabious) that faces south, southwest or southeast, and one that is often located behind a tussock of sheltering grass such as Purple Moor-grass (*Molinia caerulea*) or scrub, sometimes gorse, heather or Bog Myrtle (*Myrica gale*). The shelter is sometimes provided by a rise in the ground. The Marsh Fritillary also uses south facing banks or the south or west facing side of a hummock as ovipositing sites. On exposed west facing Succisa-rich grassy slopes, Marsh Fritillaries lay on sheltered plants near the base of the slope. North facing slopes are never used. Plants selected for egg laying vary from large prominent plants to fairly small plants, some not developed enough to flower, consisting of just 5 or 6 basal leaves. The female curves her abdomen onto the underside of a long leaf that enjoys full sunshine. Females only lay in sunny conditions. It takes about 50 minutes to lay her eggs, which are glued in neat rows to the leaf's underside. One captive female laid 317 eggs on 4th

Freshly laid Marsh Fritillary eggs on underside of Devil's-bit Scabious leaf

June 1998 and lived long enough to mature and lay a second batch of 204 eggs on 11th June. Second batches are always smaller than first batches.

Marsh Fritillary eggs can take over thirty days to hatch. The earliest hatched larvae found in the wild in 2007 were on 22nd July but most do not hatch until August. When they first hatch larvae spin a web on the underside of the leaf and feed on the mesophyll. The tiny larvae are stubby and brown with a conspicuous black head. Feeding damage is a good guide to the presence of the larvae with affected leaves a pale, sickly brown. The larvae then desert the leaf and spin two fresh leaves together and feed inside their nest. This lends protection from enemies including two parasites that live exclusively on the Marsh Fritillary caterpillars, *Apanteles bignelli* and *Apanteles melitaearum*. Larvae are vulnerable when they leave to spin a new protective web and ground-dwelling spiders must consume a large number.

The older the larvae the more leaves they bind together. When a plant's leaves are eaten, the whole nest of caterpillars moves together to an adjoining plant. This explains why females never lay on isolated plants There must be adjoining foodplants for the larvae to migrate to quickly and easily. By the third moult the larvae are ready to hibernate. By early October almost all larval nests are hibernaculum nests and these are usually located beneath vegetation and are extraordinarily difficult to find. However, on wetter sites such as Dunshane Common in County Kildare hibernacula are located in vegetation, about 170mm above the ground. By this stage larvae are black and have more obvious bristles. The hibernaculum is a much denser web than that spun by feeding caterpillars.

Larvae become active again in February. At this time of year air temperatures are often low so larvae must leave the protection of the larval webs and gather together in black masses to bask, in order to absorb as much heat and sunlight as possible in order to digest their food. Basking takes place on dry vegetation such as on clumps of Purple Moor-grass or on webs. Older caterpillars bask in smaller groups, and eventually alone. By mid-April larvae are black with a white stripe down the centre of the back and flanks. Larvae also have white specks along the body. From about April 20th caterpillars start to reach their full size. At this stage larvae have been found feeding on Honeysuckle (*Lonicera periclymenum*) and captive larvae

Marsh Fritillary larvae basking in spring

Marsh Fritillary pupa on Devil's-bit Scabious leaf

will also accept this plant. Some literature states that the larval stage does not extend beyond April but healthy larvae have been observed pupating early in the second week in May. Larvae have been observed feeding up to 23rd May in 2007. However, it is likely that parasitic Apanteles wasps have infected these larvae and their larval stage is being deliberately prolonged in order that the parasite, which cannot infect eggs or adult butterflies, will emerge as an adult wasp at the same time as the next generation of Marsh Fritillary larvae hatch. There is considerable variation in the size of fully grown caterpillars: they range in length from 25-30mm. This may reflect the sex of the larvae.

Marsh Fritillaries mating: female left, male right

Larvae pupate on grass stalks, heather and directly on the foodplant, even on the upperside of the scabious leaf. The chrysalis is attached to the leaf by a silken pad on the abdomen. It is an attractive pupa, pale grey in colour with rows of bright yellow spots decorating the abdomen. Dark blotches adorn the wing cases. Like the larvae, pupae range in length, from 11-15mm. This reflects the considerable size difference between the sexes. One final detail about the adult is worth mentioning. Virgin females can be distinguished from mated females. Mated females have two tan coloured bald patches on the underside of the abdomen at the tip. This indicates mating as the males seals the sexual organs to deny other males access to ensure that his genes are passed on.

The Marsh Fritillary is declining in Ireland. The distribution maps from the *Millennium Atlas 2000* show that it is now absent from the southeast, and from the south and east coasts, excepting Counties Down and Antrim in Northern Ireland. In Northern Ireland colonies exist in Counties Down (eight colonies), Antrim (two colonies) Tyrone (at Golan Big) and Fermanagh (ten colonies, including nine new populations found in 2007). It is found in a few sites in the southwest and a small number of sites in the Burren. It is found in the area south of Ennis in County Clare and in Counties Galway, Roscommon, Sligo, Donegal, Kildare (four colonies), Offaly, Tipperary and Cork. However, most sites are quite small and the species is very local. It also has a meta-population structure, meaning that it has a central population with outlying colonies that are lost during the periodic declines which are characteristic of this butterfly's ecology, and which are then re-occupied during periods of expansion. This means that the Marsh Fritillary's large colonies must be protected and also that corridors to outlying areas must be preserved, which involves protecting the landscape. This is a considerable challenge. Another vital factor is the need for grazing management. Without a network of managed habitats, isolation of populations will spell doom for this largely sedentary, short-lived butterfly.

Speckled Wood Breacfhéileacán Coille
(Pararge aegeria)

Male Speckled Wood (first generation)

The Speckled Wood is a dark brown butterfly with cream coloured spots. The spring generation from the overwintered pupa has larger spots that are a richer cream than those of the summer generation. Males are easily distinguished from females by their smaller size (47mm wingspan, 50mm for females), the smaller size of their cream spots and their combative conduct. Males fight other males for territory. These fights consist of spiralling in close circles, battles that often see the butterflies drifting across a glade or road. When engaged in territorial disputes they are oblivious to danger and can be struck by traffic or snatched by Spotted Flycatchers (*Muscicapa striata*) or dragonflies. The territory being fought over is usually in a sunny glade or part of a ride bathed in sunlight with good perching points, such as a bramble bush or Hawthorn hedge. It is classically a butterfly of dappled sunlight, found where sunshine penetrates leaf cover to create dappled light on the ground.

Males have two mate-seeking strategies. One is to patrol back and forth over its sun filled glade and the other is to perch and wait for a female to pass by. Males perch on wooden fence posts, rocks or leaves, usually the latter. Like most species, females are less conspicuous, except when laying eggs. The Speckled Wood rarely visits flowers, although it has been observed feeding on Wild Carrot. It feeds mostly on aphid honeydew. It is the most shade tolerant of all our butterflies but is absent from dark woodland floors. It can be seen between late April and mid-October, (it has three broods) apart from a two-week gap in July. Owing to the presence of many stretches of wild bushy hedgerows growing at the sides of narrow country roads and wild grasses at the bases of the hedgerows, this is one of our most common and widespread butterflies and is our most abundant woodland species.

Female Speckled Wood (spring generation)

The female Speckled Wood comes to your notice when ovipositing. She flutters around large vigorous tussocks of Cock's-foot (*Dactylis glomerata*) or Couch Grass (*Agropyron repens*), lays a single bun-shaped yellow egg on the underside of a leaf and then departs. Egg laying takes place in summer in shaded, humid locations while in spring and autumn more open, sunny sites are chosen for ovipositing.

The egg hatches within two weeks and summer generation larvae, which are the same hue as their foodplant, reach full size within four weeks. It pupates on a grass stalk or even low down on a stone wall. The pupa is a lovely apple-green colour and lasts for four weeks in summer. This species hibernates from October as a pupa or larva.

The Speckled Wood is very common throughout Ireland except in urban areas where there is no habitat. It is found where tall, lush, humid grasses with some shade present. The only areas it is not recorded from are parts of the west coast. This is a general countryside butterfly and will readily breed in appropriately managed rural and suburban gardens.

Cock's-foot Grass, larval foodplant of Speckled Wood

Wall Brown Donnóg an Bhalla
(Lasiommata megera)

Male Wall Brown

This butterfly is popularly called the Wall. Males are smaller than females and have a deeper orange colour and a broad brown bar across the forewings. Males are up to 53mm in wingspan and females 55mm, but both sexes are often smaller. It has two generations a year, in May/June and August. The second generation is more abundant. This is a sun-worshipper and is found on stony pathways along cliff tops, woodland rides, dunes, stony lakeshores, rocky outcrops on mountains, bare peat on cutaway bogs and limestone pavement. Walkers usually flush it, and then it flies ahead and settles, only to be dislodged again. A male perches or patrols in search of a mate like the Speckled Wood. It feeds on the nectar of umbellifers like Wild Carrot but is not an avid feeder.

The female lays on grass clumps abutting a bare warm area of stone, sand or peat. The eggs are laid on Cock's-foot, Yorkshire Fog (*Holcus lanatus*) and Common Bent (*Agrostis tenuis*), among others. The whitish egg hatches after one to two weeks. The green larva completes its development in four weeks during the summer. The green pupa lasts about two weeks in summer and seven months when it overwinters. The Wall also overwinters in the larval stage.

The Wall seems to have years of abundance and scarcity. In some years it is hardly seen, while in others it is highly conspicuous. While not a butterfly of the general countryside,

Female Wall Brown basking on limestone

individuals do occasionally migrate across unfavourable terrain. When doing so it abandons its usual habit of pausing to bask or feed and continues purposefully on, flying at about 1¼ metres above the ground. It is found throughout most of Ireland, except for Northern Ireland where it has recently declined. Here it is found chiefly along the County Down coastline, but is hardly found anywhere else in the northeast. Elsewhere in Ireland, it is found all around the coast, including the County Donegal coast. There are many inland localities except for north County Cork and the south Ulster counties. However the most reliable sites for this insect are coastal areas.

FAMILY - SATYRIDAE
Grayling Glasán
(Hipparchia semele subspecies hibernica/
Hipparchia semele subspecies clarensis)

Grayling on limestone-*hibernica* form

Graylings are large elusive butterflies and are masters of disguise. One moment a Grayling obtrudes dramatically on your notice, opening large tawny wings and just as quickly it has melted into the sandy or rocky terrain. A glimpse at the photograph will convey its natural camouflage. Another facet of its disguise lies in the ability to align itself to avoid casting a shadow. There are bright tawny patches on the uppersides of its forewings and hindwings and it always rests with closed wings. When flying it seems to hold itself in a "V". The breeze that is usually evident in the exposed habitats favoured by this creature seemingly carries it. It has one brood, flying from late June to early September. The sexes are similar except that males (56 mm wingspan) are smaller than females (61 mm). It is not an active feeder but in very hot weather large numbers can gather to feed on Creeping Thistle, (brambles, heather and Thyme.

Females lay a spherical white egg singly on a range of fine grasses such as Sheep's- fescue (*Festuca ovina*), while coastal populations feed on Marram (*Ammophila arenaria*). Sparse short patchy swards are preferred for egg laying. Larvae hatch within three weeks and are

Clarensis form of Grayling

pale brown with darker brown and yellow stripes. This provides an excellent blend with the sand or with the pale straw-coloured grasses of late summer and autumn. They hibernate after two months and resume feeding in spring, completing their development in June. The pupa, which is formed below ground, is typically blunt at both head and tail, tan in colour and lasts about a month.

The Grayling is present in Ireland in two forms. The subspecies *clarensis* is a much paler form occurring in the Burren while *hibernica* is found elsewhere in Ireland. It is found around most of the coast and throughout the Burren. It also occurs inland and is probably overlooked. It can be discovered in some unlikely situations. This is a butterfly of hot, dry, dusty places and yet it has been found in a County Wicklow bog at a rocky outcrop where drier conditions prevail. Colonies vary enormously in size with very small numbers on small dune systems and large numbers on extensive dunes such as those in Brittas Bay, County Wicklow. It is common in parts of the Burren on exposed limestone pavement and on limestone pavement with an abundant but not uniform cover of Hazel scrub such as at Coole/Garryland, County Galway on the western side of Coole Turlough in the Dunowen townland.

FAMILY - SATYRIDAE
Hedge Brown/Gatekeeper Geatóir
(Pyronia tithonus)

Male Hedge Brown on bramble

The Hedge Brown butterfly is also called the Gatekeeper. It is on the wing from late July to early September. Its upperwing surfaces are brown with rich orange patches. The female's forewings have a clear orange patch, while the male's forewings have a clear brown patch extending into this orange patch from the base of its forewing. The male is noticeably smaller, measuring 44mm across the forewings, while the female can measure up to 48mm. The species is nearly always associated with scattered scrub or native hedgerow with wild grasses growing at the edges. It also inhabits open woodland, like that found at The Raven, County Wexford. Males patrol along pathways near hedges or along hedges and turn at a certain point and retrace their flight path. Females spend more time perching, basking and feeding on nectar. On warm, sheltered sites they can reach enormous numbers, feeding during hot conditions on Creeping Thistle and bramble. They often congregate to feed on flowers growing at a break in a hedge or where a long hedgerow with flowering bramble ends and is adjoined by tall wild grassland. Butterflies vanish when the sun disappears and seek out the underside of bramble leaves.

Egg laying is inconspicuous and the reason is that eggs are simply ejected in flight. They are dropped where grass clumps adjoin patches of scrub or hedgerows. The bun-shaped egg, which undergoes colour changes from yellow to white (with rusty markings) to greyish brown, hatches after three weeks to yield a greenish larva with a yellow lateral stripe, which overwinters and resumes feeding in March, forming a pupa in June. The butterfly emerges after a month.

Female Hedge Brown on bramble

Mating pair

The Hedge Brown is found in the south of Counties Kerry, Cork, Kilkenny, Tipperary, Waterford, and Wexford and at three locations on the County Wicklow coast and inland in County Wicklow. Its restricted distribution in Ireland is unusual as it has expanded its range much further inland and much further north in Britain. It is also on the verge of re-colonising Scotland if it has not already done so. This expansion is probably in response to climate change. What may be preventing its spread inland in Ireland may be unsuitable habitat factors. This butterfly is not very mobile and intensively farmed areas in Counties Cork, Waterford, Wexford and the coastal plain in County Wicklow may be the blocking problem.

FAMILY - SATYRIDAE
Meadow Brown Donnóg Fhéir
(Maniola jurtina subspecies *iernes/*
Maniola jurtina subspecies *insularis)*

Female Meadow Brown on umbellifer

The Meadow Brown is probably Ireland's most abundant butterfly. Males are smaller than females (52mm wingspan males, 56mm females). Females have more extensive orange patches on the forewings but otherwise sexes look similar. From examining specimens found in Ireland, it looks as though *Maniola jurtina insularis,* the subspecies found in Britain, is also found here – the diagnostic feature being that the *insularis* male has only a small, faint orange tinge around and below the eye-spot on the forewing. This butterfly is present where there are wild grasses and wild flowers. It is not found on intact bogs (except in transit) or on high mountains or dense woodland. Its flight period is long, (it is single- brooded) extending from the second week of June to mid-September. Its long emergence period is probably because the egg-laying period extends from late June to September. Interestingly it appears to have a longer or later emergence period in parts of the west of Ireland. The butterfly's flight period is all but over in late August in County Kildare while along the Burren and Donegal coasts an abundance of freshly emerged Meadow Browns will be found. This may be linked with longer development periods for the larvae on windswept grasslands. The species is an avid feeder on thistles, Common Knapweed and even Buddleia.

Bi-pupilled form of Meadow Brown-a common variation found in this butterfly

Both sexes bask and fly with an up-and-down bobbing flight, powered by short flicks of the wings. This is a general countryside species and migrating individuals are regularly seen crossing unsuitable habitat. Females generally remain on the ground until found by a male. Males spend considerable time in the air seeking females. Males even fly in light rain provided it is humid. Mating pairs are frequently seen in long grass.

Females can sometimes be seen in patches of short grass, walking around twitching, as though nervous or excited. This behaviour could be a 'testing' exercise, checking for suitable grass species on which to lay eggs, tasting with taste receptors on the feet. Some eggs are laid directly on grass while others are squirted out in flight, something that can be seen in bright sunlight.

The bun-shaped egg is yellow with brown blotches and hatches after two weeks. The hairy green larva has a yellow lateral stripe and feeds on Perennial Rye-grass, meadow grasses (*Poa* ssp), bents, and when older in May, Cock's-foot. Pupation occurs in June. The green pupa, which may have dark stripes, lasts up to a month.

Meadow Browns can survive in isolated colonies for long periods of time. A colony in South County Dublin survived on about a hectare of wild grassland that was cut off from other suitable habitats for a decade. The Meadow Brown's response to having the optimum conditions – a sunny, sheltered, extensive grassy habitat with tall and short sward and rich nectar sources - is to produce spectacular numbers.

The Meadow Brown is a widespread and abundant butterfly in Ireland. It is probably more numerous than the Green-veined White but not quite as widespread.

FAMILY - SATYRIDAE
Ringlet Fáinneog
(Aphantopus hyperantus)

Ringlet

The Ringlet is one of our most common butterflies. The sexes are very similar except that the males have darker upper surfaces. Freshly emerged males are almost black on their upper surfaces. The wingspan is 42-48mm for males and 46-52mm for females. It flies from mid-late June to mid-August with a peak in July. This is a general countryside butterfly associated with lush, rank grassland with scrub, hedges and/or woodland edges. In short, it needs shaded but vigorous grasses. Much of Ireland has damp grassland so it is very common here.

It is usually encountered as a quiet, undemonstrative creature, bobbing up and down in a slow gentle flight among tussocky grassland in mid-July. The male stays airborne for considerable periods as it searches for a female perched on grassland vegetation. Paired butterflies can often be seen perched on stalks low down in the sward. The Ringlet likes to feed on brambles, thistles (and orchids, especially Pyramidal Orchid (*Anacamptis pyramidalis*). An

Male Ringlet basking

Ringlet larva on Cock's-foot Grass

interesting feature is its ability to fly in damp drizzly conditions while other butterflies are grounded.

Females lay eggs in flight or by releasing them into the air while perched on a grass blade. The dome-shaped egg is yellow, later pale brown. It hatches after two weeks and the larva is beige with a cream coloured lateral stripe and has stubble on its skin. It probably eats a variety

Female Ringlet basking on Bracken

of grasses and as Cock's-foot is very abundant on its sites this is probably the main plant used. The caterpillar hibernates and resumes feeding when temperatures rise in March. The pupa appears in June and is beige with small dark blotches. It has a blunt head and broad, cone-shaped abdomen and is similar in shape to the pupa of the Grayling. This stage lasts two weeks.

This butterfly is found throughout Ireland and will breed in rural gardens if correctly managed for this peaceful butterfly.

Small Heath Fraochán Beag
(Coenonympha pamphilus)

Small Heath

An active, tawny, bright little Satyrid (member of the brown family) bobbing around its open country grasslands is the impression bestowed by this species. Males and females look very similar but females are larger and less active than males (male wingspan 33mm, female wingspan 37mm). There seems to be some variation in the size of this species. Two sites studied in County Kildare sustain healthy populations but individuals found on the more open, more extensive site were noticeably larger than those on the smaller site. The smaller site also had more scrub but both have plenty of nectar sources. Both sexes rest with closed wings. It double-brooded and on the wing from mid-May/June and August/mid-September. It occurs throughout Ireland but is absent from many inland areas. It prefers drier, better-drained grassland than the Ringlet and Meadow Brown. The larval foodplants are fescues meadow grasses and bents. It is found on sand dunes, machair, limestone grassland, drier parts of cutaway bogs and upland sites.

Males often perch on low shrubs and chase other males away. Sometimes a female appears and attracts a number of eager males. Copulation occurs on grassland vegetation. Females lay their whitish, spherical eggs singly on grass blades and these hatch after two weeks. The larva is apple green with darker green dorsal and lateral lines. Larvae that over-winter complete their growth by the end of April. The pupa, which is similar in size to the Speckled Wood's, is pale green with black streaks and last about three weeks.

This species appears to be less widely distributed in Ireland that in Britain. Despite having many inland colonies, especially in Munster, its strongholds are the coasts. One possible reason for these differences in distribution is that more recording effort is concentrated along the coasts. A second reason is that its preferences are for drier habitats, which are found in coastal areas. It is not a fen/wet bog butterfly and this excludes it from large areas of wetland. Yet a drier area of a wet meadow will often have a colony of Small Heath. It also dislikes rank grassland and an absence of grazing on heavier soils does not favour it. It is certainly not the ubiquitous species it is described as being in Britain.

FAMILY - SATYRIDAE
Large Heath Fraochán Mór
(Coenonympha tullia)

Large Heath on raised bog

The Large Heath is almost exclusively found in wet bogs, which are its only reliable habitat. It is very occasionally found in wet fen grassland. It looks like a larger version of the Small Heath. Males and females are similar in size with the wingspan ranging from 35-40mm in both sexes. Males' upper surfaces are slightly darker than those of the female. Its upper surfaces are orange-brown. There are two colour forms in Ireland, the polydama form occurs in the midlands and has more conspicuous spotting on its underwings and the scotica form occurs in the northwest, west and south and this form is paler with fewer spots. These separate forms occur within individual sites. The flight period lasts from the first week in June to early August.

They are found in wet extensive lowland bogs with an abundance of the larval foodplant, Hare's–tail Cottongrass (*Eriophorum vaginatum*). On these sites huge populations can develop. One can see the butterflies bobbing up and down almost a metre above the bog surface. On cold cloudy days it does not take flight but a search of Cross-leaved Heather (*Erica tetralix*) usually flushes out an adult. It will leap up, bounce arbitrarily along, as though at the complete mercy of the breeze, and then tuck itself back into the heather. On poor habitats with low populations, males will patrol an area for long periods flying back and forth in search of a mate. Usually females are readily located on the bog vegetation. Like the Small Heath, it always rests with closed wings and is almost always perched in a slanted position to absorb sunlight.

The yellow cone-shaped egg is laid at the base of a tussock of the foodplant and hatches within two weeks. The larva is dark green with two distinct yellow stripes on its flanks. The caterpillar over-winters and pupates in June. It forms an attractive dark green pupa with bold black stripes on its wing cases. The chrysalis stage lasts about three weeks.

It is a simple matter to check for this species. One must visit a wet bog in early June or July on a warm day. The distribution of the Large Heath mirrors the presence of intact lowland and upland bog. It is found in the midlands, west, northwest and southwest and is probably under-recorded. It does not occur on badly damaged bogs or cutaway bogs and it is vulnerable to local extinction due to the destruction of bogs. There are nature reserves where habitat protection should ensure its continued survival. It is important to exercise vigilance however. On Girley Bog, near Athboy, County Meath, drains were dug despite its protected status.

Hare's-tail Cottongrass (*Eriophorum vaginatum*) - larval foodplant at Bunduff, County Sligo

Such an action would, if not stopped, destroy a Large Heath colony. Behaviour like this should always be reported to the Irish Peatland Conservation Council and to the National Parks and Wildlife Service office in the county concerned.

Female Large Heath on spearwort

Rare migrant species

A small number of butterfly species resident in Europe occasionally appear in Ireland during the summer and autumn. Most of these have a migratory tendency. The species that have been recorded here are: **Pale Clouded Yellow** Buíóg Liath (*Colias hyale*), resident in southern Europe; **Bath White** Bánóg Bhath (*Pontia daplidice*), resident in southern Europe; **American Painted Lady** Áilleán Meiriceánach (*Cynthia virginiensis*), resident in the Canary Islands; **Camberwell Beauty** Bé na Fallainge (*Nymphalis antiopa*) resident in northern France; **Queen of Spain Fritillary** Fritileán Niamhrach (*Issoria lathonia*) resident in northern France and the **Monarch** Bleacht Fhéileacán (*Danaus plexippus*), resident in southern Iberia, Canary Islands and North America. Records for all of the above are very few in number. The most frequently recorded is the Monarch and its large size (wingspan over 100 mm) probably accounts for its notability. All of the rare migrants species are chiefly recorded along the south and the east coasts.

New species

Three new species have recently been recorded in Ireland. The three species are the Essex Skipper (*Thymelicus lineola*), Small Skipper (*Thymelicus sylvestris*) and the Comma (*polygonia c-album*). They are common in Britain and Europe. It remains to be seen whether these species survive here in the long term.

Essex Skipper Scipeálaí Essex
(Thymelicus lineola)

Female Essex Skipper

The Essex Skipper with a wingspan of 26-30mm is slightly smaller than the Small Skipper, from which it is almost indistinguishable unless it is caught and its antennae are examined. The Essex Skipper has black tips on its antennae club's undersides while the Small Skipper has orange or orange-brown or brown on the under surface of its antennae clubs. The upper surfaces of the forewings and hindwings are golden. The male is distinguished from the female by a prominent black line, called the sex brand, on the forewing. Its flight period begins later than the Small Skipper's. On the County Kildare site where both species occur the first Essex Skippers appear at the end of the third week in July (in County Wexford it emerges during the second week in July) and the flight period extends into the second half of August. However freshly emerged individuals can be found in late August. It nectars on Common Knapweed, Red Clover, hawkbits, and thistles. It is eye-catching as the males flutter through grasses with wings flashing gold in sunlight. Females become more active in the afternoon when the day's hottest period has passed and this is when most egg laying occurs. Its eggs are laid in small batches and are inserted into the leaf sheath of Cock's-foot. The cream coloured eggs hatch in April and the green larva, which has parallel yellow stripes on its flanks, completes its growth in June and forms a long slim yellow pupa. This lasts about three weeks. This butterfly is currently established in County Kildare and on several sites in County Wexford.

Small Skipper Scipeálaí Beag
(Thymelicus sylvestris)

Male Small Skipper

This butterfly measures 27-34mm across the wings with females slightly larger than males. It looks very similar to the Essex Skipper, on its upper surfaces and undersides. The underside of its hindwing has a greenish tinge and the underside of the forewing is orange. The antennae undersides differ from those of the Essex Skipper. Its flight period differs somewhat also: in County Kildare it emerges during the second week in July and can still be easily found in the second week in August. It has been seen as late as the August 21st. It nectars on the same flowers as the Essex Skipper and lays its eggs in the same manner by inserting them into a grass sheath. However, it chooses a different species of grass, Yorkshire Fog and its eggs hatch before winter, unlike those of the Essex Skipper.

Its habits and habitat requirements are similar to those of the Essex Skipper. This grassland species requires an abundance of its foodplant and nectar sources. It nectars on Bird's-foot-trefoil, Common Knapweed, Red Clover, hawkbits and thistles. It prefers ungrazed, but not rank grassland as these conditions result in a loss of wild flowers. The Small Skipper also prefers some shelter and is less common on windswept grasslands. It settles readily when the sun is obscured and appears just as speedily when its rays return. Males adopt patrolling and perching in their search for females. Ovipositing females flutter around the seed heads of grass to check that it is Yorkshire Fog before alighting on the grass stalk. She inserts the eggs in the gap between the stalk and leaf sheath.

The eggs hatch after three weeks and larvae hibernate. Caterpillars become active in April and complete their growth in June. The pupa is very similar to the Essex Skipper's. This stage lasts two weeks. Like the Essex Skipper it is a species of considerable character. Males bob and

Female Small Skipper

weave through grasses, their wings glinting gold in the sunshine as they seek a mate. A wild dash occurs if it sees another golden insect and it is a challenge for the eye to follow.

The Small Skipper has been found breeding on a site in County Kildare since 2005.While it is too early to say if it will become established in Ireland this butterfly appears to be thriving and spreading.

Yorkshire Fog - larval foodplant of Small Skipper

Comma Camóg
(Polygonia c-album)

Comma basking on Bracken

This striking butterfly has a wingspan of 50-64mm, with males smaller than females. It can be confused with the Small Tortoiseshell or fritillary in flight but when settled its oak-leaf scalloped wing edges render it unmistakeable. The Comma derives its name from the white 'comma' mark on the underside of the hind wing. It has a flight pattern similar to the Small Tortoiseshell and inhabits the sunny edges of woods, lanes and ventures into gardens located near woodland.

The complex brood structure bears a superficial resemblance to that of the Small Tortoiseshell except it has a partial second brood in late August and September. The second brood along with some of the first brood individuals that did not breed hibernate on tree roots among fallen leaves in wooded areas. The butterfly emerges in March/April. Its main larval foodplant is the Stinging Nettle but unlike the Small Tortoiseshell, the larva is solitary. It resembles a black and white bird's dropping and when young it feeds on the underside of the upper leaves of the foodplant. When fully grown it is a handsome caterpillar with light orange lateral markings and conspicuous spikes. Its pupa is brown and hangs beneath a nettle leaf. The adult emerges after two weeks and feeds on the nectar of bramble and frequently basks on bramble leaves and Bracken.

Underside of Comma – note comma mark on centre of hindwing

There is an indication that this species may be about to colonise Ireland. It has been seen in Counties Down (1997,1998), Kilkenny (2002), Wexford (2007,2008) and Kildare (2007). These occurrences, while mainly of single individuals, imitates the pattern noted when it re-colonised central, eastern and northern England since World War I and when it recently colonised the Isle of Man. Breeding has been confirmed in Scotland (2006). It seems a matter of time before breeding is confirmed here and its establishment as a permanent resident could soon follow.

Introduction to Site Guide

The sites are grouped alphabetically under county headings. The Discovery Series map that the site is found on is given. Each site is grid referenced and its habitats are described. For selected sites a full species list is provided to ensure you know where to find all the native butterflies. Where (a) appears after a species in the list given for a site this indicates that the butterfly is abundant on the site. For other sites some key species are listed and the rest are for you to discover. This is surely part of the challenge and enjoyment of exploring the countryside. Ownership of sites is indicated where known. No difficulty gaining entry to any of the sites was encountered. Most are nature reserves or other areas (like coastal sites) that enjoy free public access. If in doubt always seek the permission of the landowner. The challenges/difficulties in crossing the terrain are also described (where these exist).

Visit sites in good weather from late April to mid-September. Without warmth and sunshine your quest is likely to yield little other than disappointment. The ideal conditions for observing butterflies consist of dry conditions with little wind. The optimal times to observe butterflies is between 10.45am and 3.45pm but during excellent sunny weather searching between 10am and 5pm will be productive. You must be aware of the flight periods of individual butterfly species described in the species accounts. The flight periods are subject to prevailing weather and prolonged unseasonable weather will affect emergence times to some extent. Finally, please note that species distribution can change and the information given in the site guide is correct as of 2008.

Mill Lane, Palmerstown, Dublin 20

Location map

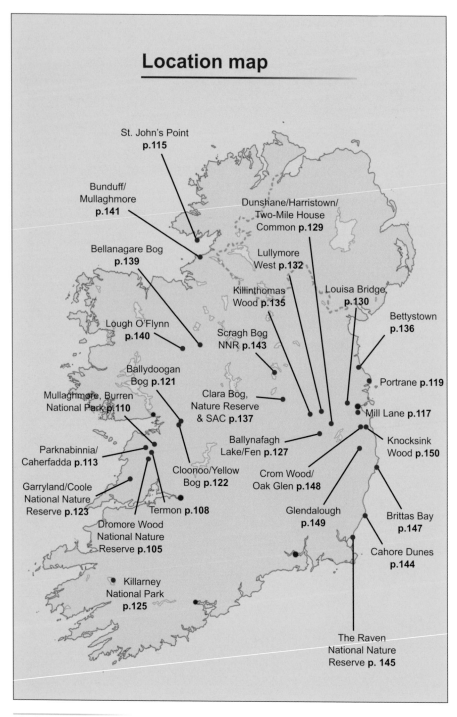

St. John's Point **p.115**

Bunduff/ Mullaghmore **p.141**

Dunshane/Harristown/ Two-Mile House Common **p.129**

Bellanagare Bog **p.139**

Lullymore West **p.132**

Killinthomas Wood **p.135**

Louisa Bridge **p.130**

Bettystown **p.136**

Lough O'Flynn **p.140**

Scragh Bog NNR **p.143**

Ballydoogan Bog **p.121**

Portrane **p.119**

Mullaghmore, Burren National Park **p.110**

Clara Bog, Nature Reserve & SAC **p.137**

Mill Lane **p.117**

Parknabinnia/ Caherfadda **p.113**

Ballynafagh Lake/Fen **p.127**

Knocksink Wood **p.150**

Cloonoo/Yellow Bog **p.122**

Crom Wood/ Oak Glen **p.148**

Garryland/Coole National Nature Reserve **p.123**

Termon **p.108**

Glendalough **p.149**

Brittas Bay **p.147**

Dromore Wood National Nature Reserve **p.105**

Cahore Dunes **p.144**

Killarney National Park **p.125**

The Raven National Nature Reserve **p. 145**

Dromore Wood National Nature Reserve, County Clare

Discovery Series 57, Grid reference R354 864

Dromore Wood

The most productive parts of Dromore Wood for butterflies are the clearings, along tracks, areas of scrub and riverbanks. This species-rich woodland contains a number of habitats. These include rivers, lakes, turloughs, flooded meadows, limestone pavement and reed beds. The list of butterflies found here is:

Wood White (*L. sinapis* or *reali* or both?)
Brimstone (a)
Large White
Green-veined White (a)
Orange-tip (a)

Brown Hairstreak
Purple Hairstreak
Small Copper
Common Blue (a)
Holly Blue

Small Tortoiseshell
Peacock (a)
Red Admiral
Painted Lady
Silver-washed Fritillary

Speckled Wood
Meadow Brown
Ringlet (a)

Dromore Wood

This area contains diverse woodland. The main tree species are oak, Ash, Wild Cherry (*Prunus avium*), Holly, Hazel, Spindle (*Euonymus europaeus*), Common or Purging Buckthorn, Yew (*Taxus baccata*), Elder, Blackthorn, Hawthorn and Wild Crab Apple (*Malus sylvestris*), as well as non-natives such as Norway Spruce (*Picea abies*). In spring parts of the woodland floor are carpeted with Bluebells (*Hyacinthoides non-scripta*). Areas around the banks of the River Fergus have wet grassland with wetland wild flowers such as Kingcups (*Caltha palustris*). Rocky outcrops appear in various places including the 'Castle Trail' walking route. Here flowers typical of limestone pavement occur.

The wood holds a remarkable population of Brimstone butterflies and this is especially evident during May and August. Over forty were recorded along the main road into the wood on 24th August 2000. Part of the reserve lies to the east of the local road that divides the woodland and a large population of Brimstones can be found here. The site may be the best location in Ireland for these elegant, eye-catching butterflies. The low-growing wetland vegetation around the banks of the Fergus River, on the east side of the reserve, is a good location for Green-veined Whites, Orange-tips and Common Blues, while muddy spots are places to look for male Holly Blues in hot weather. Clearings in the woods are where Wood Whites, Speckled Woods, Silver-washed Fritillaries, Peacocks, Small Tortoiseshells and Brown

Male Brown Hairstreak on Bracken

Hairstreaks are concentrated. The nettle bed behind the small visitor centre that is located in the main part of the wood is a good place to look for Peacock and Small Tortoiseshell caterpillars.

Dromore is important for a number of other creatures. It has a number of bat species including rare species such as the Lesser Horseshoe Bat (*Rhinolophus hipposideros*). A range of bird species is found, including Heron (*Ardea cinerea*), Sparrowhawk (*Accipiter nisus*), Blackcap (*Sylvia atricapilla*) and many more. Pine Marten (*Martes martes*), Badger (*Meles meles*) and Fox also occur. This wood shares a number of similarities with Garryland Wood near Coole, in County Galway. The main differences are that Garryland has more limestone pavement and the Grayling occurs there. Dromore is more aesthetically pleasing and has better access, tracks and a visitor centre that has recently (2008) being upgraded.

Directions: For Dromore take the Ennis Road (R476) from Corofin. Just under 2km from Corofin turn left onto the L1098 to Ruan. Drive just over 5km to Ruan. Dromore is signposted from Ruan (turn left on main street). It is a little over 2km from Ruan.

Termon, County Clare

Discovery Series 51, Grid reference M299 013

Termon

This site is located along the left side of the road not far to the north of the Burren Perfumery. The site is part of an SAC and is open and unfenced. The following species are found here:

Dingy Skipper (a)	Small Tortoiseshell
	Peacock (a)
Wood White (a)	Red Admiral
Clouded Yellow	Painted Lady
Brimstone	Pearl-bordered Fritillary (a)
Green-veined White	Dark Green Fritillary (a)
	Marsh Fritillary (a)
Small Copper	Speckled Wood (a)
Small Blue	Wall Brown (a)
Common Blue (a)	Grayling (a)
Holly Blue	Meadow Brown (a)
	Ringlet (a)
	Small Heath (a)

The area where the Marsh Fritillary breeds is only 280m x 90m in extent (see grid reference) and is very interesting botanically as it contains an intimate mixture of limestone grassland flora and wetland flora. Devil's-bit Scabious, Purple-moor Grass, heathers (*Erica* ssp) and Tormentil occur along with Spring Gentian (*Gentiana verna*), Bloody Cranesbill (*Geranium sanguineum*), Mountain Avens (*Dryas octopetala*), Water Avens (*Geum rivale*), Thyme,

Goldenrod (*Solidago virgaurea*), Bellflower (*Campanula rotundifolia*) and Bird's-foot-trefoil creating a beautiful spectacle. Some limestone and a small stream is present here. The site also supports a high population of the Dark Green Fritillary with twenty-six individuals counted in a five minute period in early July 2008. Although not the richest butterfly site in the Burren the area has wonderful peace and beauty. One feels it is tucked secretly away and it is a gem that is unspoilt.

Marsh fritillary/Dark Green Fritillary habitat at Termon

At the northern end of the site walk about 20 metres and you will see a sign for St Fiachtna's Well. Walk through the gap in the wall into a series of clearings in the Hazel scrub and enjoy the limestone grassland and pavement with its typical butterfly species such as the ubiquitous Common Blue, Grayling, Wall Brown and Small Heath amongst others. Continue your journey until you reach a beautiful wet meadow with a different hue of green to that among the limestone – a soft subtle olive green spangled with the white of orchids in summer and Grass of Parnassus (*Parnassus palustris*) in August. Here, especially in early summer, Green-veined Whites are encountered. Banks of Hazel and high ground rise powerfully above this meadow as if to cradle it.

When you leave, the whole experience is one you will certainly bring with you. Try Cassidy's restaurant in nearby Carran to complete your visit. Caution is advised due to uneven ground.

Directions: Take the R476 from Corofin, pass through Kilnaboy and drive north for just over 4km. Turn right at Leamaneh Castle onto the R480. Continue on the R480 for 2.5km and take the right turn onto the third class road that is signposted for Carran village. Turn right at the national school in Carran. A short distance past the UCG Field Research Station turn to the left and continue until you see the sign for St. Fiachtna's Well. The Marsh Fritillary colony is c.20m south of this sign, back along the road you travelled. Explore the wetlands and pavement in this area on the St. Fiachtna's Well side of the road. Instead of driving from Carran you can park outside Cassidy's pub and walk the 2.5km to the site.

Mullaghmore, Burren National Park, County Clare

Discovery Series 51/52, Grid reference R304 945

Mullaghmore

This is the richest butterfly site in Ireland and given its fairly modest size one of the best in Britain and Ireland. The following species have been recorded:

Dingy Skipper (a)	Small Tortoiseshell (a)
	Peacock (a)
Wood White (a)	Red Admiral
Clouded Yellow	Painted Lady
Brimstone (a)	Pearl-bordered Fritillary (a)
Small White	Dark Green Fritillary (a)
Green-veined White	Silver-washed Fritillary
Orange-tip	Marsh Fritillary
Brown Hairstreak (a)	Speckled Wood (a)
Small Copper	Wall Brown (a)
Small Blue (a)	Grayling (a)
Common Blue (a)	Meadow Brown (a)
Holly Blue (a)	Ringlet (a)
	Small Heath (a)

The habitats that support this range (and abundance) of butterflies include limestone pavement, limestone grassland, scrub, wet grassland, (at Rinnamona Lough at R297 943), wet meadows on deeper soils and traditionally managed hay meadows.

The grasslands are extensively grazed in winter and spring and the hay meadows are cut in September, with the hay removed to ensure a continuation of low soil fertility that favours wild flowers. The grassland at Rinnamona Lough, which supports the Marsh Fritillary, is lightly grazed by cattle. Some of the low-lying wet meadows flood in winter and spring and are grazed by cattle in late spring. Thus natural succession is held in abeyance and open habitats are preserved. Hedgerows and patches of scrub shelter the area creating an ideal microclimate for butterflies and a wealth of other insects.

Should time be pressing, and you can only visit one butterfly site, let this be it. Not only is it rewarding for the abundance and range of the butterfly fauna, the floral display is also remarkable. In late April the profuse flowering of violets, Spring Gentians and Primroses is breathtaking. Although violets and Primroses are common in Ireland, the abundance here is stunning and the effect must be witnessed to be appreciated. The meadow immediately south of the crossroads at R 304 945 is a fascinating example of superabundance. In June the display of Ox-eye Daisies is so dazzling that the field looks as though it is cloaked in snow!

Spring Gentians, a Burren speciality

The limestone grasslands and hay meadows play host to a succession of spring and summer wild flowers and any visit between late April and early September really is a delight. The grasslands are rich with both wetland orchids and dry grassland orchids evident. From late June orchids are especially glorious and these attract the attention of striking butterflies such as the Dark Green Fritillary. An excellent area to search for the Pearl-bordered Fritillary is the limestone grassland and scrub on both sides of the L1112 road leading to the crossroads. Should you turn right at the crossroads and head towards Lough Gealain the scrub and clearings to the left provide excellent opportunities to watch this rare butterfly. A walk along the Green Road is also productive for the Pearl-bordered Fritillary and several other butterflies.

Further on is a gate giving access to some wonderful hay meadows at Gortlecka (R 308 950). The grass here is teeming with frogs in June, so watch your step. A visit to Lough Gealain is also obligatory and fine limestone pavement and heath, inhabited by Walls and Graylings, opens before you and the view here is incomparable. Alder Buckthorn and Purging Buckthorn grow together near the lake, a rare circumstance in Ireland. To the west of the lake is a raised area of limestone pavement and a collapse hollow here contains a large pond. This is a wonderfully secluded spot where Brimstones breed in abundance. An Alder Buckthorn plant was found here draped over a limestone rock peppered with Brimstone eggs in May. Caution is advised due to uneven ground. The entire area is of great interest and you will certainly enjoy exploring here.

Bee Orchid found at Mullaghmore

Directions: The gateway village to the south of the Burren is Corofin. Take the R476 north from Corofin to Kilnaboy. At Kilnaboy post office, turn right onto the third class road (L1112). Continue straight for 4.7km until you reach the pull in point before a small crossroads at Gortlecka. (Signposted Green Road). Park here and explore the meadows on your right as a good starting point.

Parknabinnia/Caherfadda, County Clare
Discovery Series 51, Grid reference R262 943

Parknabinnia/Caherfadda

This SAC comprises c100 hectares of limestone pavement, limestone grassland and scrub. A large number of species have been recorded here:

Dingy Skipper (a)	Small Tortoiseshell
	Peacock
Wood White (a)	Red Admiral
Clouded Yellow	Painted Lady
Brimstone	Pearl-bordered Fritillary
Large White	Dark Green Fritillary (a)
Small White	Silver-washed Fritillary
Green-veined White	Marsh Fritillary (a)
	Speckled Wood (a)
Small Copper	Wall Brown
Small Blue?	Grayling
Common Blue (a)	Meadow Brown (a)
	Ringlet
	Small Heath (a)

This is a beautiful area located above the village of Kilnaboy, near Parknabinnia Wedge Tomb. The area has the largest colony of Marsh Fritillary recorded in the Burren. The colony extends over large areas of the west facing slopes. The butterfly is found on both sides of the road. If you are looking for larval nests in late August a good area to search is near the base of the slopes near the scrub (R260 935).

Apart from an abundance of butterfly species this is a picturesque site and its openness confers a sense of freedom. The herb-rich turf is alive with colour. It boasts many of the Burren's wild flowers growing at a high density including Bloody Cranesbill, Burnet Rose, (*Rosa pimpinellifolia*) Bird's-foot-trefoil, Harebell and various orchids. Cattle grazing maintains the grassland. Caution is advised due to very uneven ground.

Limestone grassland at Parknabinnia

Directions: Travel north from Corofin on the R476 and drive through Kilnaboy village. Continue along the road for 1km and take the first right turn (L5096) after the village. Continue carefully downhill along the L5096 and soon you will start climbing. After a steep climb you emerge from Hazel scrub zone and you will see the wedge tomb on your left. Drive on until you reach an open area. Park here and explore the slopes, especially those on the left hand side of the road (i.e. downhill).

St. John's Point, County Donegal

Discovery Series 10, Grid reference G715 695

St. John's Point

This is a coastal promontory in southwest Donegal, where limestone grassland is found at its southern tip. It appears to be underlain in places by sandstone where acidic, boggy conditions feature. This is a lovely site to walk and is easily accessible. Signs ask you not to park on the sward and with good reason. It is a special botanically rich site, similar to the Burren. The limestone flora consist of plants such as Bloody Cranesbill, Cowslip and Kidney Vetch, but acid-loving plants are to be found close by including Meadow Thistle and Meadowsweet (*Filipendula ulmaria*). There are wonderful sea and coastal views to be enjoyed together with some rare butterflies, including the Marsh Fritillary and Small Blue. The Grayling is also found here in good numbers and is, interestingly for a site with a good deal of bare limestone, not the *clarensis* form found in the Burren but the *hibernica* form found elsewhere in Ireland. There is a remarkable population of Meadow Browns and one hundred and ninety-four individuals, including three mating pairs were recorded on a visit on 8th August 2007.

St. John's Point is very unspoilt and extensive cattle grazing maintain its richness. Caution is advised due to uneven ground and cliffs. Another site which is relatively close by and worth visiting is Sheskinmore, grid reference G 7096. This site lies 5km north of Ardara and is reached by taking the R261 (Ardara/Portnoo road). This is a beautiful machair and wetland site that is very productive for butterflies.

Limestone and wild flowers at St John's Point

Directions: Travelling northwards take the N56 at Donegal town. Go through Dunkineely and take the first left after the end of the 50km speed limit. St. John's Point is signposted at this left turn. Continue carefully on this narrow road until you reach gates at the southern tip of the peninsula. Park here (beside the beach) and enter the site over the cattle grid. The site has a narrow road that terminates at the lighthouse.

Mill Lane, Palmerstown, County Dublin

Discovery Series 50, Grid reference O 086 356

Mill Lane

Mill Lane is located on the southern banks of the River Liffey, east of the Westlink Bridge on the M50 and west of Mill Lane (below Stewarts Hospital). The following species have been recorded:

Réal's Wood White
Clouded Yellow
Large White
Small White
Green-veined White (a)
Orange-tip (a)

Small Copper
Common Blue (a)
Holly Blue

Small Tortoiseshell (a)
Peacock
Red Admiral (a)
Painted Lady (a)
Silver-washed Fritillary

Speckled Wood (a)

Meadow Brown (a)
Ringlet (a)

South Dublin County Council is currently developing this site as a linear park; it has walkways and banks of native trees have been planted. A network of fields divided by hedgerows tumbles downhill towards the River Liffey. Scrub and rough rank grasses occur and the wetter areas with patches of reeds occur near the river. The most interesting part of the habitat is two wet meadows at the eastern end of the site. An old iron bridge crosses the Liffey at this point. Here flower-rich meadows play host to all the species listed for the site. A particularly note-worthy aspect of the site is the presence on the eastern extremity of an area of wetland flowers, notably Ragged Robin, Purple Loosestrife and Flowering Rush (*Butomus umbellatus*). This is an excellent place to observe the life cycle of the Small Tortoiseshell because the nettle beds are in a warm sheltered location and mating behaviour is easily observed. The fields above have good populations of Meadow Browns and Ringlets both of which nectar on thistles. The Ivy and Holly around the ruined church attract the Holly Blue, while the tussocky grassland nearby favours the Common Blue. Orange-tips and Green-veined Whites prefer damp areas near the river while in mid-summer the Vanessids (Small Tortoiseshell, Peacock, Red Admiral and Painted Lady) and the Cabbage Whites (Small and Large Whites) can be readily observed nectaring on the nearest Buddleia growing on the western part of the site.

It is heartening to know that, just below Ireland's most congested roadway on the threshold of the capital city, some of our butterflies have a place where they can live in abundance and peace and enhance the lives of the city's inhabitants.

Directions: Travelling from Dublin City take the N4 west and turn right at the crossroads at the pedestrian bridge in Palmerstown. Take the next left, then the next right. Drive to the end of this cul-de-sac and the site lies in front of you. Buses 25,26,66 and 67 from Pearse Street near Trinity College will bring you to Palmerstown. The site is called Palmerston Lower on the O.S. map.

Portrane, County Dublin

Discovery Series 43, Grid reference O 254 515

Portrane

This coastal site consists of a beach and narrow sand dune system. The butterflies seen here are:

Large White (a)	Small Tortoiseshell (a)
Small White (a)	Red Admiral (a)
Clouded Yellow	Painted Lady
	Dark Green Fritillary
Small Copper (a)	
Small Blue (a)	
Common Blue (a)	Wall Brown
Holly Blue (in gardens beside dunes)	Grayling (a)
	Meadow Brown (a)
Small Heath (a)	

In addition, Green-veined White, Réal's Wood White and Orange-tip have been recorded nearby.

This site's great advantage is the easy accessibility together with car parking available beside the local pub. The butterflies are easy to find in the sand dunes and are often in abundance. It is an excellent site for Small Blues, a species that is very local in Ireland. The east coast, the Burren and the northwest coast are its strongholds. Portrane has a thriving colony, breeding on Kidney Vetch, the species only foodplant. Here it has an abundance of Bird's-foot-trefoil and Kidney Vetch to use as nectar sources. The dunes provide plenty of shelter and warmth needed by this diminutive butterfly. This shelter has diminished due to recent erosion. The Small Blue is at its most abundant from late May until about mid- June so plan to visit during this period if you can. The colony extends to the Rush sand dunes on the northeast side of the Rogerstown Estuary.

Portrane

Flying amongst the Small Blues in early June are Small Heath, Wall Brown, Large White, Small White, Clouded Yellow, Common Blue and Small Copper, while in July you can see all of the other species listed. For those of you disinclined to exertion, this is an excellent site to visit.

Directions: From the M 1 north of Swords, take the road for Donabate / Portrane.Go through Donabate village to Portrane on the coast. Trains run from Connolly Station, Dublin to Donabate and bus 33B runs from Swords in County Dublin. All of the species listed can be found about 20 metres to the left of the entry to the dunes accessed from the side of "The Brook" public house.

Ballydoogan Bog, Loughrea, County Galway

Discovery Series 52, Grid reference M 672 180

Ballydoogan Bog

This is a cutover bog with some intact bogland. The site also contains scrub, woodland and grassland. Parts of the site have deep ditches and very uneven ground, so caution is advised. It escaped becoming a landfill site and the local people are keenly aware of the site's significance for nature. The area is particularly well known for its large Marsh Fritillary colony. Nineteen butterfly species have been recorded including Silver-washed Fritillary, Réal's Wood White, Small Copper, Common Blue and Speckled Wood. The notable absentee is the Small Heath, a species usually found on Marsh Fritillary sites. Wellington boots are needed.

Directions: Ballydoogan Bog is east of Loughrea. Travel 5km on the N6 from Loughrea Turn right off the N6 onto the N65 (signposted Portumna). Proceed for about ½ km until you see the bog on your left.

Sundew (*Drosera* ssp) growing amongst sphagnum on Ballydoogan Bog

Cloonoo/Yellow Bog, Loughrea, County Galway

Discovery Series 52, Grid reference M 585 175

Cloonoo/Yellow Bog

This site lies alongside the south side of the N6 Loughrea-Galway road. It has no designation and is in private ownership, yet it is one of the most extensive known sites for Marsh Fritillary in Ireland. The site comprises about 40 hectares. In August/September the area looks purple due to the blossoming Devil's-bit Scabious. While the site has never been systematically counted for the Marsh Fritillary larval nests over sixty nests were found in just three of the fields. Most of the site has suitable habitat for Marsh Fritillary. Two donkeys graze the habitat. It has a diverse and rich wetland flora hosting plants characteristic of acidic and alkaline conditions. A number of butterfly species occur on the site but the sheer numbers of Marsh Fritillary highlight its importance. Wellington boots are needed.

Directions: From Loughrea, take the N6 for Galway. Travel for about 3.5kms (2 miles) from the end of the 50km/hour zone. The site is on the left, with Loughrea behind you. You will notice a conifer plantation on the right hand side of the road where there is a small area for parking. Inquire locally regarding access.

Garryland/Coole National Nature Reserve, County Galway

Discovery Series 52
Garryland Grid reference M411 035
Coole Grid reference M437 045

Garryland

These sites have a range of habitats types such as semi-natural woodland, scrub, hedgerows, limestone pavement, grassland and turloughs. The butterflies found here are listed.

Wood White	
Large White	Small Tortoiseshell
Brimstone (a)	Peacock (a)
Green-veined White	Red Admiral
Orange-tip	Painted Lady
	Pearl-bordered Fritillary
	Silver-washed Fritillary (a)
Purple Hairstreak	
Small Copper	
Common Blue (a)	Speckled Wood (a)
Holly Blue (a)	Wall Brown
	Grayling (a)
	Meadow Brown
	Ringlet
	Small Heath

Graylings mating, male on left

It is possible that the Brown Hairstreak is found here as it occurs close by. This is an excellent site for the Silver-washed Fritillary especially in sunny rides. The Brimstone is very common here although not as abundant as in Dromore Wood. It is a good site for Odonates (dragonflies) that prey on the butterflies found here.

The wood ends quite abruptly and is adjacent to an area of short grassland (this is flooded in winter) and an area of limestone pavement. This area is botanically diverse and is noted for its Juniper (*Juniperus communis*), Yew, Rowan (*Sorbus aucuparia*), Ash, oak, Holly and some fine specimens of an endemic tree, Irish Whitebeam (*Sorbus hibernica*). The mammal fauna includes the Pine Marten, Stoat, Fox, Red Squirrel (*Sciurus vulgaris*), Field Mouse (*Apodemus sylvaticus*), Badger and Bank Vole (*Clethrionomys glareolus*).

This is a large site and includes the largely non-native woodland at Coole where there is an excellent visitor centre which features a good audio-visual presentation (free of charge) detailing the habitats and wildlife of the area as well as restaurant and restroom facilities. Caution is advised when visiting the limestone pavement due to uneven ground.

Directions: To reach Coole take the Galway Road (N 18) and travel north from Gort. Coole is about 1 km outside Gort on the left and is clearly signposted. The Garryland Wood side of the reserve is more difficult to find. Take the R460 Corofin road from Gort and turn right at the Kilmacduagh monastic site. Continue on the third class road for 4km and you will arrive at Garryland Wood, which is on the right hand side. A track leads into the woods from here.

Killarney National Park, County Kerry

Discovery Series 78, Grid reference V 908 863

Killarney National Park

The park comprises of over 10,000 hectares of woodland, lakes, bogs and grassland. The list of butterflies that occur in the park is as follows:

Réal's Wood White/Wood White	Small Tortoiseshell (a)
Clouded Yellow	Peacock (a)
Brimstone	Red Admiral (a)
Large White (a)	Painted Lady
Small White (a)	Silver-washed Fritillary (a)
Green-veined White (a)	Marsh Fritillary (probably extinct)
Orange-tip (a)	
	Speckled Wood (a)
	Wall Brown
Green Hairstreak (a)	Grayling (a)
Purple Hairstreak	Meadow Brown
Common Blue (a)	Ringlet (a)
Small Copper (a)	Small Heath (a)
Holly Blue (a)	Large Heath

This is one of Ireland's most famous landscapes but despite its large size and its total species count of 25, it is not as rich as parts of the Burren. Some areas of the park have low butterfly numbers and species. The interior of the oak woods, high mountains and lowland bogs are unrewarding to the butterfly seeker. The most productive areas are the lowland areas around Lough Leane. The best areas for butterflies in the park are Muckross Peninsula (V 908 863) and Derrycunihy (V 908 808). Tomies Wood (V 908 893) has Green Hairstreaks and Purple Hairstreaks, while the area near Looscaunnagh Lough (V 890 796) has Grayling and Large Heath. Rocky outcrops that occur along the roadside between Muckross and Looscaunnagh Lough are also Grayling habitat.

Muckross

Directions: To get to Muckross Peninsula take the N71 southwards from Killarney for 4km and follow the signs for Muckross House. There are excellent parking, restaurant and restroom facilities. Follow the walking trails from Muckross House to Muckross Peninsula. A minor road leaves the N71 after Muckross Friary (leaves N71 at V 978 868) and goes through the peninsula. It rejoins the 'mainland' at Dinish Island, another good butterfly spot.

Ballynafagh Lake/Fen, County Kildare
Discovery Series 49, Grid reference N 810 280

Ballinafagh Lake

This site contains a number of habitat types including reed beds, fen, raised bog, rough grassland, woodland, scrub and a small area of calcareous grassland. Butterflies found here include:

Dingy Skipper	Small Tortoiseshell (a)
	Peacock (a)
Réal's Wood White (a)	Red Admiral (a)
Green-veined White (a)	Marsh Fritillary (extinct from 2000,
Orange-tip (a)	reintroduced 2006)
Green Hairstreak	Speckled Wood (a)
Small Copper (a)	Meadow Brown
Common Blue (a)	Ringlet
Holly Blue	Small Heath

This site is owned by Kildare County Council and is a candidate SAC. It has a shallow lake and is one of Ireland's premier Odonate sites. The butterflies here are not faring as well as they might. This is due to the long absence of grazing that has resulted in the development of rank grassland and scrub, which is overwhelming the flora. Another factor is the trampling and flattening of vegetation important to butterflies (especially for the Marsh Fritillary) by fishermen and their tents. Following a recent report to the wildlife service these issues should be addressed.

Nevertheless the site is very attractive, especially in May/early June and August when the floral and butterfly display is at its best. The site has a number of orchid species as well as local plants such as Marsh Cinquefoil (*Potentilla palustris*). Caution is advised due to presence of water. Wellington boots are required.

Directions: Travelling from Clane, turn right at the church in Prosperous and continue, carefully, down the third class road for 3 km. Turn left at the 3 km mark (at grid reference N 822 298). Drive for about 1 km, pass a large house, "Whooper's Path", and enter the car park on your left. The best butterfly areas are around the lakeshore.

Dunshane/Harristown/Two-Mile House Common, County Kildare

Discovery Series 55, Grid reference N 880 128

Dunshane

This is a wetland site few naturalists are aware of. It has elements of bogland, calcareous flushes, wet and dry grassland. It is quite a large site (c.40 hectares) and is open and exposed. Extensive cattle grazing maintain the attractive flora and butterfly habitats.

The site has a range of orchids, Grass of Parnassus, Common Knapweed, Bird's-foot-trefoil, Devil's-bit Scabious, Cuckoo Flower, Water-cress and rank and fine grasses. There is a strong Marsh Fritillary population and a large population of Small Heath. Interestingly, the Small Heath butterflies that live here are large individuals. The site is an important reservoir for butterflies in an area of pleasant but bland countryside. The surrounding moraines consist chiefly of grazing land and there are a number of stud farms in the general area. The site has much uneven ground and is edged by ditches containing water, so access is a little difficult. Use the gates at either end of the site. Rubber boots are required.

Directions: Take the Kilcullen Road from Naas (R 448) for 6km. Turn left at the Sidegate Cross Roads (just before a thatched cottage). After about 30m turn left onto a third class road. The Common is about 100m ahead, on both sides of the third class road. Park near the GAA football grounds.

Louisa Bridge, Leixlip, County Kildare

Discovery Series 50, Grid reference O 992 368

Louisa Bridge

This SAC is primarily a calcareous spring-fed wetland site sandwiched between the Intel site and the Grand Canal at the train station in Leixlip. The site lies mainly on the north bank of the Rye River. Kildare County Council owns the site and considerable improvements to the site are planned. This will include a boardwalk and steps on the southern side of the river, near the waterfall. Although the number of species found here is modest the populations are large. The Réal's Wood White and the Holly Blue are especially common. The following species have been recorded here:

Réal's Wood White (a)	Small Tortoiseshell (a)
Large White	Peacock (a)
Small White	Red Admiral
Green-veined White (a)	Painted Lady
Orange-tip (a)	
	Speckled Wood (a)
Small Copper	Meadow Brown
Common Blue (a)	Ringlet
Holly Blue (a)	

It is also a good site for wetland orchids, dragonflies and Smooth Newts (*Triturus vulgaris*). The canal bank walk is interesting for its butterflies and flora. The hedgerows here are excellent for Holly Blue and mating and egg laying can easily be observed. Caution is advised due to presence of water.

Kingcups on the bank of the Rye River

Directions: Take the N4 west from Dublin and turn onto the R148 at the sign for Leixlip. Drive through Leixlip village on the R148 until you reach the train station at Louisa Bridge. There is a car park opposite the station (parking fee applies). The site is about 100m east of Louisa Bridge, between the Intel factory complex to your left and the canal to your right, with the bridge at your back. The train from Connolly Station in Dublin takes you here as does the no.66 bus from Pearse Street, Dublin.

Lullymore West, County Kildare

Discovery Series 49, Grid reference N 694 295

Lullymore West

This is one of the most important butterfly sites in the east of Ireland in terms of the number of species recorded and in terms of population sizes. Thirteen of the twenty-two species recorded are abundant. The list contains the following species:

Dingy Skipper (a)	Small Tortoiseshell (a)
	Peacock (a)
Réal's Wood White (a)	Red Admiral (a)
Clouded yellow	Painted Lady
Brimstone	Dark Green Fritillary
Large White	Silver Washed Fritillary
Small White	Marsh Fritillary (a)
Green-veined White (a)	
Orange-tip (a)	Speckled Wood (a)
	Wall Brown
Small Copper	Meadow Brown
Common Blue (a)	Ringlet (a)
Holly Blue	Small Heath (a)

The site is c.25 hectares in total and is in divided ownership. The Irish Peatland Conservation Council (IPCC) own about 5 hectares and Bord na Móna own the remainder.

The site is unusual in some ways. It is really a degraded habitat. It was once an intact raised bog that has been completely destroyed. It was worked over twenty years ago but the thin bare layer of peaty substrate has been colonised by various herbaceous plants, mosses, shrubs and trees and a wonderful mosaic of habitat types have developed. These include orchid rich grassland, calcareous grassland (underlain by marl), a wetland dominated by mosses and wetland wild flowers, willow scrub, birch woodland and bare patches of peat.

Topographical features shelter the area. It is below the level of a track and raised bog remnant with a conifer plantation and tall birch trees to shelter it. Thus it enjoys a calm, sheltered microclimate. The other unusual characteristic is the large number of butterfly species recorded from this inland site. The best butterfly sites in Ireland are usually those on limestone or in coastal areas with good dune systems and machair grassland. The site is comparable with rich sites in the Burren.

At the start of the main butterfly flight season in April the site can appear dreary and uninspiring. Spring indeed seems to arrive late here. Given a sustained period of sunshine Brimstones, Orange-tips, Green-veined Whites, Peacocks, Small Tortoiseshells and Speckled Woods soon appear and the site becomes a spectacle. Brimstones seem to hug the woodland edge while Orange-tips patrol the grasslands, especially damper areas, while Green-veined Whites flutter around the more open grassland. Let the sun be obscured and everything returns to its resting place. By May vast changes are obvious and more butterflies are added to the list. Réal's Wood Whites fly over the track leading to the site and around the tussocky

Devil's-bit Scabious at Lullymore

grasslands adjoining scrub and trees. Marsh Fritillaries appear on the grassland. Dingy Skippers buzz in and out of view. Small Coppers flash deep gold before settling on a Cuckoo Flower to feed or on bare peat to absorb sunshine.

The site is especially important for its Marsh Fritillary colony, which was first recorded in the early 1990's but which probably existed before then. Interestingly its parasite(s), *Apanteles Bignelli* and/or *Apanteles melitaearum*, is/are also present. This is a sign that the butterfly has been established here for some time. The parasite is seen as important to the species maintenance. There are records of Marsh Fritillary population explosions, which resulted in mass starvation when the larvae had defoliated all of the Devil's-bit Scabious. The presence of the parasite on the site is likely to prevent this.

The site has an important flora with some rare plants. These include Alder Buckthorn and Wintergreen (*Pyrola rotundifolia*). There are a large number of orchid species here. A large number of moth species have been recorded, including the Narrow-bordered Bee Hawk (*Hemaris tityus*) moth that breeds here. This species has become increasingly rare in Britain and Ireland and this eastern Irish site is therefore important for this moth.

This site is worth a visit from late April to late September. The site to the right of the track is owned and managed for the butterfly fauna by the IPCC, so their permission must be sought prior to entry onto the site. Bord Na Mona owns the area to the left. Horseflies inhabit the site but it is more or less free of these until about mid-June. After this prepare for them by dressing to cover arms and legs, and wear a hat. Caution is advised due to uneven ground. Wellington boots are needed.

Directions: From Allenwood (N 760 226) take the R 414 west and cross Shee Bridge 1km on the left (drive slowly here). Continue straight on for c. 4km and you will reach the Irish Peatland Conservation Council centre (signposted Bog of Allen Nature Centre). Turn right at the centre and continue down the third class road until you reach a T-junction (at N 704 263). Turn left onto this rough track and continue slowly, until you reach a bend that has an industrial railway track (N 696 260). Park here. You will see a track leading to the site. Walk to the end of this track and the site is straight in front of you. The land to the right of the track is in the IPCC's ownership. Bord Na Mona owns that to the left. Check with the IPCC (045-860133) before entering the site.

Killinthomas Wood, County Kildare

Discovery Series 49/55, Grid reference N 667 218

Bluebells at Killinthomas Wood

This Coillte (Irish forestry service) site is renowned locally for its display of Bluebells in April and early May. It is worth visiting for this alone. Butterflies recorded here include Brimstone, Large White, Green-veined White, Orange-tip, Peacock, Holly Blue and Speckled Wood. It has an attractive ground flora including Wild Garlic or Ramsons (*Allium ursinum*), Primroses, Common Dog-violets and Lady's Smock.

The tracks through the wood (especially the wide track from the car park) are good for butterflies bathed as they are in sunlight and enjoying the shelter provided by the woodland. The wood itself also hosts Red Squirrel. The wood is mainly deciduous, with Beech, Wych Elm (*Ulmus glabra*), Hazel, Ash, oak, Holly and Yew.

Directions: The wood is signposted from the Main Street in Rathangan. Take the R 401 and continue to the small roundabout at the end of the village. Turn right off the roundabout. Drive for about 2km and you will find a right turn to Killinthomas Wood. There is a car park, benches and picnic tables.

Bettystown, County Meath

Discovery Series 43, Grid reference O 162 750

Dunes at Bettystown

This beach and dune system (SAC) is very popular and people walk here all year round. A sample grid reference for the dune system is O 162 750.

The butterflies are found mainly in the dunes but migration to the southeast can be observed on the beach in late August and September, especially involving Red Admirals. Large and Small Whites can also be seen on the beach itself. Perhaps these are migrating too?

The dune system becomes more expansive as you travel north towards Mornington. The Dark Green Fritillary, Common Blue and Small Heath all occur. The dunes contain an impressive array of wild flowers including Thyme, orchids, trefoils and clovers and many others. Altogether the dunes are an impressive escape from the mass suburbia overwhelming this general area.

Directions: From Dublin's M50 take the M 1 for Belfast. Go about 36km and take the exit for Julianstown. Pass through Julianstown village and turn right onto the R 150 for Laytown. Continue along the coast road (R151) until you reach Bettystown village. Park in the village, if possible, and go to the beach. The dune system is on your left.

Clara Bog, Nature Reserve & SAC, County Offaly

Discovery Series 48, Grid reference N 245 305

Clara Bog

Clara Bog is the largest and most intact raised bog in the Irish midlands. The following butterfly species have been recorded here:

Réal's Wood White (a)	Small Tortoiseshell (a)
Brimstone	Peacock (a)
Large White	Red Admiral
Small White	Painted Lady
Green-veined White (a)	Silver-washed Fritillary
Orange-tip (a)	Marsh Fritillary (not presently found here)
Green Hairstreak (a)	Speckled Wood (a)
Small Copper	Wall Brown
Common Blue	Meadow Brown (a)
	Ringlet
	Small Heath (a)
	Large Heath (a)

The most productive areas of Clara Bog are the margins along the sides of the road that bisects the bog. Other good areas are along the tracks leading into the bog near where the bog margin stops hugging the road. Another excellent area is a flower rich meadow (at grid reference N 245 305) on the left hand side of the road with Clara village at your back. In June Green Hairstreaks can be found around the scrub at the edge of the bog along the roadside. Tap the Hawthorn and chances are you will dislodge a couple. If they see each other and both are males, a battle is sure to follow. Stand back and observe their antics and approach quietly and you will get a close view. This butterfly can also be seen on the bog and on the birch growing

Peacock nectaring on Devil's-bit Scabious

on the bog margins. Should you arrive early between 9am and 10am in early June, observe the tussocky road verges for freshly emerging Réal's Wood Whites. It is not unusual to see them clambering up stalks as they prepare to dry their wings. Orange-tips and Brimstones are also in evidence, flying close to the bog woodland. In late June the Silver-washed Fritillary occurs near the wood edge while Large Heaths – literally in their hundreds- are present on the bog surface. This is a most reliable site for this declining butterfly. The track on the right hand side that goes in to the bog is particularly interesting because it contains calcareous material, possibly derived from a local esker. It supports lime-loving plants such as Marjoram, Bird's-foot-trefoil and Quaking Grass. Here Small Heaths, Common Blues, Réal's Wood Whites, Meadow Browns and Ringlets are found. Some old abandoned dwellings have clumps of Stinging Nettle and these nourish Small Tortoiseshell and Peacock larvae, while common grassland butterflies may be seen in the flower rich meadow which lies a few metres up the main road from which the track runs into the bog. This is also where the Marsh Fritillary last bred.

When visiting Clara Bog you must exercise care. There are deep drains and uneven ground. Most of the butterflies can be observed from the road verges and tracks, while a marked track leading on to the bog surface, on the left hand side of the road, is a good place for viewing the Large Heath. The flora is interesting, especially the orchids and columbines that bloom on the track margins on the left hand side. Curlews, Merlin, Kestrel and Meadow Pipits nest here and a Short-eared Owl was seen here in 2005. Boora Parklands at Taraun is well worth checking, as Bord na Móna manages the area for its wildlife. Wellington boots are needed for both sites.

Directions: Clara Bog lies 2 km south of Clara town in north County Offaly; on either side of the road to Rahan. The turn from Clara to the bog is well signposted.

Bellanagare Bog, County Roscommon

Discovery Series 32, Grid reference M 710 826

Bellanagare Bog

This is a large raised bog, much of which is intact. The site is designated as an SAC. The site has several streams and tracks onto the bog provide good access. The bog, which has a well-developed dome, is quite wet and difficult to cross. It is an outstanding site for the Large Heath (*polydama* form) that emerges here in early June. Other species of note include Réal's Wood White and Small Heath, with large populations of Peacocks in August. All of the butterflies are clearly visible from the tracks leading into the bog.

I recommend two tracks. A track can be found on the Frenchpark to Castlerea road. This is located at the foot of a small hill, just past a very charming old cottage. You can park on the track and walk into the bog from here. The track terminates at the NPWS signage. Another track is located off the Ballanagare to Castlerea road and it brings you deep into the bog. The tracks are themselves of considerable interest, rich in wild flowers, insect and bird life. Caution is advised due to uneven ground and Wellington boots are needed.

Directions: From Dublin take the N4 to Longford, followed by the N5 to Frenchpark. In Frenchpark, turn left onto the R381 for Castlerea and continue on this road until you leave the forestry behind you and the bog opens up on both sides of the road.

Lough O'Flynn, County Roscommon

Discovery Series 32 & 39,Grid reference M 590 795

Lough O'Flynn

This is an angling lake well known for its Brown Trout. It is a calcareous lake and the chief interest for butterflies lies on the western and eastern shores where fascinating and diverse vegetation is found. On the western shore, dry calcareous-loving plants such as Kidney Vetch thrive only feet away from wetland plants like Marsh Cinquefoil. This diversity is mirrored in the butterflies found here. This SAC has Marsh Fritillary and Small Blue. The latter breed on steep east facing slopes. The route recommended if walking the western shore, takes you from wet, Succisa-rich grassland on the western shoreline to the bog at the northwestern side of the lake. Wellington boots are needed for the western shore.

It must be emphasised that the western shoreline is physically demanding. Boots are vital and several fences and drains have to be negotiated. The eastern shore is much easier to traverse and has a large Marsh Fritillary population.

Directions: From Castlerea take the N60 to Ballinlough. Go through Ballinlough, taking the Ballyhaunis Road. Immediately outside Ballinlough, just past a petrol station, turn right. Proceed for about 1.25km and pull in. The lakeshore lies below and you should walk down to the shoreline and along it, heading north. You will soon reach the steep slopes, which hold the Small Blue colony. The Marsh Fritillary colony is found along this shore as well as a number of other grassland/wet grassland species.

To access the eastern shoreline take the road from Ballinlough to Loughglinn. The lake will soon become visible and a track leads down to it.

Bunduff/Mullaghmore, County Sligo

Discovery Series 16, Grid reference G 710 555

Bunduff Lough

This site consists of dunes, machair, alkaline fens, rough grazing and a Maritime Pine plantation. The following butterflies are known from the area:

Dingy Skipper	Small Tortoiseshell
	Peacock (a)
Réal's Wood White	Red Admiral
Clouded Yellow	Painted Lady (a)
Large White	Dark Green Fritillary
Small White	Marsh Fritillary (a)
Green-veined White (a)	
Orange-tip (a)	Speckled Wood
	Wall Brown
Small Copper	Meadow Brown
Small Blue (a)	
Ringlet	Small Heath (a)
Common Blue (a)	Large Heath

The site (an SAC for machair) has a rich butterfly fauna. The reason for this diversity lies with the range of habitat types. You can walk directly from sand dunes straight onto machair (popular with walkers) then on to wet base-rich fen and cross a narrow road to flower-rich pasture.

A consequence of the closeness of different habitat types is that you will see species one would not normally find together. Thus you can observe Marsh Fritillary larvae and Graylings in flight in the same place. Usually you would have to go to widely separated localities to see both species, but here it is all laid on due to a remarkable assemblage of habitat types.

Orchids and Kidney Vetch on machair at Mullaghmore

Another outstanding feature is the wide-ranging flora. Thyme, Devil's-bit Scabious, hawkbits, Grass of Parnassus, Bird's-foot-trefoil, Ragged Robin, Common Knapweed and various orchids occur. Orchid species found at Bunduff include: Fragrant Orchid (*Gymnadenia conopsea*), Lesser Butterfly Orchid (*Platanthera bifolia*), Marsh Helleborine (*Epipactis palustris*), Common Twayblade (*Listera ovata*) and Broad-leafed Helleborine (*Epipactis helleborine*) as well as various marsh orchids (*Dactylorhiza* ssp). Cattle graze the area but some over-intensive farming activity on the opposite site of the Bunduff lakes looks to be a possible threat to the site. The grassy pasture on the landward side of the road overlooking the lakes/machair is also grazed, but here grazing seems quite light and several Marsh Fritillary larval nests were found here. Meadow Brown and Green-veined White also occur on this tussocky grassland, while Speckled Woods are encountered near the willow scrub. Common Blues are found on both sides of the road, as are Marsh Fritillaries, while Grayling, Small Blue and the Wall are found on the dunes and machair.

The site is highly recommended and the coast road around the Mullaghmore Peninsula features some lovely scenery with wild flowers in abundance especially on the seaward side of the road. There are many areas worth visiting in the general vicinity. Rosses Point, Lough Gill, Lissadell House and Drumcliff Churchyard, site of an ancient cross and final resting place of WB Yeats (note the rather cold, detached inscription on the limestone headstone) are worth a visit.

Directions: Travel north from Sligo town on the N15 and turn left at Cliffony onto the R279 for Mullaghmore. There is parking in Mullaghmore village and the site is to your right behind and among the dunes on Bunduff Strand.

Scragh Bog, National Nature Reserve, County Westmeath

Discovery Series 41, Grid reference N 420 590

Scragh Bog

This is an alkaline fen c.16 hectares and located in a shallow depression. The following butterflies are known from this site:

Réal's Wood White	Small Tortoiseshell
Brimstone	Peacock (a)
Green-veined White (a)	Red Admiral
Orange-tip (a)	Marsh Fritillary (small colony)
Small Copper	Speckled Wood (a)
Common Blue	Meadow Brown
Green Hairstreak	Ringlet
Holly Blue	Small Heath

The site has a good boardwalk and viewing platform at the northeast corner. The Marsh Fritillary is recorded as breeding close to the viewing platform. At the time of writing there is no deep water where the Marsh Fritillary breeds but this site has deep water and should never be visited alone. The track leading to the fen is an excellent area for butterflies and it is quite likely that you will see all of the species (except Marsh Fritillary) listed. Scragh Bog is an important site as it is a rare habitat type – a basin fen. It has some rare plants such as Wintergreen and the site has been much studied. It is a SAC and a nature reserve.

Directions: Travelling from Dublin take the N4 passing Mullingar and take the right hand turn at Lough Owel. The site lies about 1½ km down this small road. The right of way to the fen is through the conifer plantation located at the southeastern end of the site. There is a track leading to the site through the plantation and a sign announces the beginning of the site.

Cahore Dunes, County Wexford

Discovery Series 69, Grid reference T 215 462

Cahore Dunes

This is a lovely stretch of coastline with sand dunes. This site has similar habitats and species to those found at Brittas Bay, County Wicklow, Portrane, County Dublin and Laytown, County Meath. The beach is not crowded with visitors as it is in Laytown or Brittas. Therefore the whole experience is very pleasant. However, the latter two sites' dune systems are not very disturbed and do repay the lepidopterist and stroller alike.

The following butterflies may be found here:

Clouded Yellow	Small Tortoiseshell (a)
Large White (a)	Red Admiral
Small White (a)	Painted Lady
Green-veined White	Dark Green Fritillary
Orange-tip	
	Speckled Wood
Small Copper (a)	Wall Brown
Small Blue	Grayling
Common Blue (a)	Hedge Brown (a)
	Meadow Brown (a)
	Ringlet
	Small Heath (a)

The scrubby, tussocky dune system to the left of the car park is an excellent area for one of the site's specialities – the Hedge Brown. Late July is a good time to see them on the wing with males patiently patrolling stretches of hedgerow, scrub and trodden pathways through the Bracken. In fact you can actually follow a male keeping about 1metre behind him as he flits along the pathway seeking a mate. Very occasionally he will stop to sip on Ragwort or bramble. Moving away from the scrub to the more sandy spots you can see Graylings and, if you are lucky, a Dark Green Fritillary, dash powerfully by. Large and Small Whites are much in evidence and Small Tortoiseshells feed on nearby thistles. Small Heaths and Common Blues are conspicuous as are Cinnabar moths (*Tyria jacobaeae*) or their black and yellow striped larvae. Small Blues can also be seen in May/June. This is also a very good site for Common Lizards (*Lacerta vivipara*) probably because of the lack of disturbance. One of the great benefits of this site is its extent as you can walk long distances without encountering obstructions. The butterflies described can be readily found in the dune system, with Speckled Woods and Hedge Browns most evident near scrub.

Directions: Travelling from Dublin drive through Courtown on the R742.Take the left turn after Ballygarret village that will bring you to the dunes and there is parking at the end of this road. This area is called Old Bawn on the Discovery Series map and lies south of Cahore Point.

The Raven National Nature Reserve, County Wexford

Discovery Series 77 Grid reference T 113 265

The Raven

This reserve (an SAC) consists of open sand dunes and dunes stabilised by the planting of pine trees. The dune system is 8 km long. The butterflies recorded here are as follows:

Réal's Wood White (a)	Small Tortoiseshell
Clouded Yellow	Peacock (a)
Large White	Red Admiral (a)
Small White	Painted Lady
Green-veined White	Comma
Orange-tip	Dark Green Fritillary
	Silver-washed Fritillary (a)
Small Copper	
Small Blue (a)	Speckled Wood (a)
Common Blue (a)	Wall Brown
Holly Blue	Grayling (a)
	Hedge Brown (a)
	Meadow Brown (a)
	Ringlet
	Small Heath (a)

This is the best butterfly site on the east coast in terms of the number of species recorded. It has a number of habitats - dunes, woodland, scrub and wetland. Paths run through the woods and it is a popular site for walkers. The woods are fairly open yet sheltered producing a good Silver-washed Fritillary habitat. The scrub and open woodlands also hold a large population of Hedge Brown. There is plenty of bramble to provide nectar for woodland butterflies while the dunes also have plenty of nectar sources, especially Ragwort and Bird's-foot-trefoil. It is generally an inviting site that is good for butterflies, birds and amphibians. The Smooth Newt, Common Frog (*Rana temporaria*) and Natterjack Toad (*Bufo calamita*) all occur here.

Grayling on dunes at The Raven showing its ability to conceal itself

Directions: Take the R 742 to Curracloe. The site is signposted from Curracloe village and there is parking at the northern end. When walking towards the NPWS signage turn left to go to the sand dunes or continue straight ahead for the woodland walk. The dunes and woods are parallel so you can dip in and out of each habitat as you wish.

Brittas Bay, County Wicklow

Discovery Series 62, Grid reference T 317 845

Brittas Bay

This is a scenic bay with a fine beach and sand dunes. The beach is a major tourist attraction and is especially busy at weekends during the summer. The chief butterfly habitats are in the sand dunes that contain scrub, open sand and grassland dominated by wild flowers such as Kidney Vetch and Bird's-foot-trefoil and areas dominated by Marram Grass.

Butterflies that occur here are similar to those found just south of Cahore, County Wexford but Brittas Bay seems to have a higher population of Graylings. On hot days in August a number of males may be seen nectaring on thistles. This is somewhat unusual as the Grayling is not usually seen taking nectar and is rarely seen concentrated together in a small area. Common Blues and Small Coppers are particularly abundant. Search the northern extremity of the dunes for Small Blues. These scarce butterflies are rather local here but can be found at the northern tip of the site in early June.

Directions: Take the southbound M11 from Dublin. This becomes the N11 and from this point travel for c.49km.Brittas Bay is signposted on the left just before Jack White's pub. Turn left here and the site is 3km from the pub. There are two car parks, one at the south end and the other at the north end of the beach. Access to the dunes is from the car park. A parking fee is charged.

Common Blues mating at Brittas Bay
(male above, female below)

Crom Wood/Oak Glen, County Wicklow
Discovery Series 56,Grid reference T 173 163

Crom Wood

This Coillte (Irish forestry service) site is located on the Enniskerry Road about 4kms from the Glencree Reconciliation Centre. The butterfly interest lies alongside the track from the Crom Wood entrance all the way to the bottom of Oak Glen. The conifer part of the site was clear felled about three years ago and replanted, and the scrub evident at present should be interesting for butterflies. The species recorded include Small Copper, Common Blue, Peacock and Wall Brown. The Oak Glen was planted in the early-mid 1990's and consists of native oak, Larch, Downy Birch, alder, Rowan and Holly. This is an interesting wooded site consisting predominantly of oak - a rare plantation type in Ireland. Despite a 'deer proof' fence Sika deer have penetrated the oak wood and damaged the trees. This incursion has been reported so hopefully repairs/improvements needed will be made. The site is most interesting for butterflies in August.

Directions: Take the R115 from Rathfarnham/Willbrook/Ballyboden in County Dublin and travel towards Tallaght. The road becomes the military road after Kilakee and it takes you over the mountains of south Dublin. You will take a sharp left for Glencree at O 140 175. From the Glencree Reconciliation Centre, follow the signs for Enniskerry. Crom Wood/Oak Glen is signposted; the site is on your right.

Glendalough, County Wicklow

Discovery Series 56, Grid reference T 093 963

Glendalough

This is a wonderfully atmospheric site set in the Wicklow Mountain National Park. It contains an 8th century church and monastic settlement and these stone structures blend with the rocks, woods and lakes that are prominent in the valley. It is popular throughout the year but especially in summer. There are excellent parking facilities and walkways.

Initially it does not seem particularly rich in insect life. Indeed the open areas have fairly bland grassland, more suitable to picnicking or football playing. However a diligent searcher will find butterflies here. Silver-washed Fritillaries and members of the white and brown families occur. Perhaps the most notable species is the Grayling which occurs around the ruins of the miner's village, along the shore of the upper lake. This typically coastal species is found among the boulders and fine grasses in dry areas in what is otherwise a very wet area of the site. The visitor centre (housed in a granite cottage) located off the woodland track has an excellent display of the area's biodiversity and will be of particular interest to children. Caution is advised due to the presence of deep water.

Directions: Travelling from Dublin take the N 81 from Tallaght. Go through Blessington village and take the R 758 for Valleymount. Pass through the village of Valleymount and about 1km past the village you will see a sign for the Wicklow Gap. Keep right (the left turn is for the lake drive and Ballyknockan) and stay on this road. You will travel over the mountain road that leads to Glendalough. Alternatively, take the N11 from Dublin and look for the signs for Glendalough.

Knocksink Wood, Enniskerry, County Wicklow

Discovery Series 56, Grid reference O 184 212

Knocksink Wood

This site that contains deciduous woodland is located along the Glencullen River valley. It is a National Nature Reserve and has an environmental education centre (See www.knocksinkwood.org). The wood consists of oak/Ash/Hazel with mature willow in wet areas. The butterflies recorded are:

Large White	Small Tortoiseshell
Small White	Peacock (a)
Green-veined White	Red Admiral (a)
Orange-tip	Painted Lady
	Silver-washed Fritillary (a)
Small Copper	
Common Blue	Speckled Wood (a)
	Meadow Brown
	Ringlet (a)

There is a possibility that the Purple Hairstreak is also present as it has been seen nearby.

Knocksink Wood is attractive and accessible. There is parking, visitor facilities and walkways. The area is an excellent example of semi-natural woodland and there are few in Ireland as well developed as this. The canopy layer, under-storey, scrub and ground layers are clearly identifiable. A further reason for a visit is the wildlife garden that has been developed at the centre. This provides an excellent model of how to develop a garden for amphibians, birds and butterflies. Finally, one of our most fascinating butterflies, the Silver-washed Fritillary is abundant here.

This fritillary has a long history of occurrence and was present when the site was being developed as a nature reserve. In the late 1980's and early 1990's the tree cover was thinned by the removal of non-native conifers. This was done to restore the site to as natural a state as possible. The butterfly's response to this increased sunlight was dramatic. The population of Silver-washed Fritillaries increased and remained high for a number of years, until the cleared areas developed scrub. The butterfly has retreated to breeding along rides and pathways and wood edges where some light penetrates to the woodland floor. Accordingly courtship flights and egg laying can be observed in these areas while 'bachelor parties of immature males can be observed on Buddleia growing beside the centre and elsewhere in the wood. All of the species listed can be observed around the Education Centre and especially near and around the small clearings.

The range of butterfly species is limited as the wood grows mainly on damp, heavy, shaded soils and this limits the range of larval foodplants. Another reason is the absence of large sunny clearings filled with wild flowers. Most of the wood's butterflies rely on bramble and Buddleia for nectar with few wild flower nectar sources available here in summer. The creation of a large, sunny, sheltered clearing, especially on calcareous soil (some pockets of which occur here) would certainly yield interesting results.

Directions: Take the number 44 bus from Eden Quay to Enniskerry village. Look for the tall Roman Catholic Church spire. The entrance to the reserve is on the same side of the road as the church, on the other side of the bridge. Enniskerry can also be reached by taking the N11 from Dublin and looking for the signs for Enniskerry village.

Bibliography

Asher, Jim *et al.* (2001). *The Millennium Atlas of Butterflies of Britain and Ireland.* Oxford University Press.

Asher, *Jim et al.* (2006). *The State of Butterflies in Britain and Ireland.* Pisces Publications, Newbury.

Baines, Chris. (1985). *How To Make A Wildlife Garden.* Elm Tree Books, London.

D'Arcy, Gordon and Haywood, John. (1992). *The Natural History of the Burren.* Immel Publishing, London.

Emmet, A. Maitland and Heath, John. (eds.) (1990). *The Butterflies of Great Britain and Ireland.* Harley Books, Colchester.

Gibbons, Bob and Brough, Peter. (1992). *Photographic Guide to the Wildflowers of Britain and Northern Europe.* Hamlyn, London.

Gibbons, Bob and Gibbons, Liz. (1988). *Creating A Wildlife Garden.* Hamlyn, London.

Goodden, Robert and Gooden, Rosemary. (2002). *Butterflies of Britain and Europe.* New Holland, London.

Hickie, David (ed). (2004). *Irish Hedgerows: Networks For Nature.* Networks For Nature, Dublin.

Hickie, David and O' Toole, Mike. (2002). *Native Trees and Forests of Ireland.* Gill & Macmillan, Dublin.

Hickin, Dr. Norman. (1992). *The Butterflies of Ireland: A Field Guide.* Robert Rinehart, Cork.

Kingsbury, Noel. (1994). *The Wild Flower Garden.* R.H.S. London.

Lavery, Tim and Diane. (1990). *The Butterflies of Killarney National Park.* Government Publications Office, Dublin.

Marent, Thomas. (2008). *Butterfly A Photographic Portrait.* Dorling Kindersley, London.

Nelson, E. Charles and Walsh, Wendy. F. (1993). *Trees Of Ireland.* The Lilliput Press, Dublin.

Newland, David. (2006). *Discover Butterflies in Britain.* Wild Guides, Hampshire.

Packham, Chris. (2001). *Back Garden Nature Reserve.* New Holland, London.

Stevenson, Violet. (1985). *The Wild Garden.* Francis Lincoln, London.

Thomas, J.A and R. Lewington. (1991). *The Butterflies of Britain and Ireland.* Dorling Kindersley, London.

Thompson, Robert and Nelson, Brian. (2006). *The Butterflies and Moths of Northern Ireland.* National Museums, Northern Ireland.

Waring, Paul and Townsend, Martin. (2003). *Field Guide to the Moths of Great Britain and Ireland.* British Wildlife Publishing, Hampshire.

Websites

Belfast Naturalists' Field Club
www.habitats.org/bnfc/

Butterfly Conservation in U.K.
www.butterfly-conservation.org

Dublin Naturalists' Field Club
www.dnfc.net/www.butterflyireland.com

Galway Naturalists' Field Club
www.homepage.eircom.net/~gnfc/

Knocksink Wood National Nature Reserve
www.knocksinkwood.org

West Clare Wildlife Club
www.wcwc.ie

Wexford Naturalists' Field Club
www.wexfordnaturalist.ie

Useful Addresses

Butterfly Conservation Ireland,
Pagestown,
Maynooth,
County Kildare.
Phone (01) 6289901

Design by Nature,
Irish Wildflower Growers,
Crettyard,
Carlow,
Ireland.
Phone 353 (0) 56 444 2526
Fax 353 (0) 56 4442722
Email: Info@allgowild.com

Y.S.J. Seeds,
Kingsfield Conservation Nursery,
Broadenham Lane,
Winsham, Chard,
Somerset TA20 4JF,
England.
Phone 01460 30070
Fax 01 460 300 70
Email: ysjsseeds@aol.com

Dublin Naturalists' Field Club,
35 Nutley Park,
Dublin 4.
www.dnfc.net

Irish Peatland Conservation Council,
Lullymore,
Rathangan,
Co. Kildare,
Ireland.
Phone 353 (0) 45 860133
www.ipcc.ie